How To Develop Your Child's TEMPERAMENT

How To Develop Your Child's TEMPERAMENT

BEVERLY LA HAYE

HARVEST HOUSE PUBLISHERS
Eugene, Oregon 97402

Scripture quotations are from the *New American Standard Bible,* ©The Lockman Foundation 1960, 1962, 1963, 1968, 1971, 1972, 1973, 1975 and are used by permission.

HOW TO DEVELOP YOUR CHILD'S TEMPERAMENT

Copyright ©1977 Harvest House Publishers
Eugene, Oregon 97402

Library of Congress Catalog Card Number: 76-53068
ISBN 0-89081-034-6 Trade
ISBN 0-89081-272-1 Mass

Printed in the United States of America

DEDICATION

There has never been any question in my mind as to whom this book should be dedicated—

Linda

Larry

Lee

Lori

Our four children have been teaching us for nearly twenty-nine years. I am thankful for the temperaments that God chose for each one of them, and that He allowed us as parents to play an important role in the development of their lives.

ACKNOWLEDGEMENTS

During the writing of this manuscript I have spent the entire time traveling with my husband and speaking at Family Life Seminars in forty-six countries of the world. I greatly appreciate the assistance of my sister, Barrie Lyons, who received each chapter through the mail and took the responsibility to edit and polish until the manuscript was ready for publication. Also, many thanks to Linda English who typed and retyped until the project was done. My two married daughters, Linda and Kathy, were an added help besides my other children and grandchildren who allowed me to share many personal experiences.

TABLE OF CONTENTS

1

Children—Good, Bad, Or Indifferent

My six-year-old daughter was situated in front of the bedroom mirror and I was standing unnoticed in the hall watching her through the doorway. She had just put on one of my best dresses, a pair of high heels, and now was slipping my gloves over her little hands. I remained out of sight to watch the charade. With my white gloves on she took the lipstick and attempted to smear color on her lips. Then she picked up my hairbrush to primp, and, finally, as she was reaching for my expensive French perfume, I moved quietly into the room. I said, "My, you look lovely; and what is your name?" It was hard to keep a straight face as she looked at me because her uneven, oversized, ruby-red mouth resembled the face of a clown more than the lady she was trying to enact. She responded with surprise, "You know me! I'm Lori. Mommy, I want to be just like you."

I caught my breath and a lump rose in my throat as I realized that this child was trying to be a duplicate of me. What a responsibility! What love and adoration! What a priceless privilege to have a child who so admires her parent that she wants to be just like that parent!

God has given parents a great responsibility to love, protect, train, and discipline their children. Psalm 127:3-4 tells us that, "Lo, children are an heritage of the Lord: and the fruit of the womb is his reward. As arrows are in the hand of a mighty man, so are children of the youth.'' An arrow needs to be properly aimed or directed to reach the target. Also, the arrow requires a bow for its power and might. As I observe people who excel in the skills of the bow and arrow, I notice immediately that the bow must be brought into subjection and bent in order to properly direct the arrow. The more pliable the bow, the further the arrow will go. What a great visual aid this is to illustrate the need for parents to properly bring their children into subjection and to carefully aim and direct them toward the target.

1. *Desire Toward Evil*

A child's nature is twofold: Psalm 51:5 gives the first characteristic: ''Behold, I was shaped in iniquity; and in sin did my mother conceive me.'' This simply means that my mother who conceived me was sinful, not living in sin, but born with sin; therefore, I was born with a sinful nature also. When a child is left alone with this sin nature and not given instruction and correction, the parents can expect the results mentioned in Proverbs 29:15, ''The rod and reproof give wisdom: but a child who gets his own way brings shame to his mother.'' A child not diverted from the original condition into which he was born, will bring shame to both his mother and father. ''A foolish son is a grief to his father and bitterness to her that bare him,'' Proverbs 17:25.

I'm afraid that far too often we just endure the children for the eighteen or nineteen years they are in our care. There is great danger ahead for the child that is allowed to just grow up without any training or discipline, and there will be great sorrow and heartache ahead for the parents of such a child. Every child has the potential of becoming a delinquent and a criminal when he is left to his own ways without instruction and correction.

2. *Desire Toward Good*

Psalm 139:13-16 states, ''For thou hast possessed my reins (formed my inward parts): thou has covered me (woven me) in my mother's womb. I will praise thee; for I am fearfully and wonderfully made: marvelous are thy works; and that my soul knoweth right well. My substance (frame) was not hid from thee, when I was made in secret, and curiously (skillfully and intricately like fine needlepoint) wrought in the lowest parts of the earth (protected place). Thine eyes did see my substance, yet being imperfect (unformed), and in thy book (The Book of Life) all my members were written, which in continuance were fashioned, when as yet there was none of them.''

God oversaw the building or construction of our frames and saw that it was intricately woven together. We were designed by God. Even before we were born He went so far as to list our members and what He had planned for us in the Book of Life. It was at this time that the distinctive characteristics of our temperaments were designed before they were formed. God knew what He wanted us to be and had a plan for our lives.

However, He gave each of us a free will to choose evil or good, and the child that is not trained to choose good will undoubtedly choose evil. God knew what our natures would be and gave us many verses in the Bible to instruct us regarding evil and good. Romans 12:9b states, ''Abhor that which is evil; cleave to that which is good,'' and verse 21 states, ''Be not overcome of evil, but overcome evil with good.''

Your child's desire for evil can be related to the weaknesses of his temperament while his desire for good can be seen in the strengths of his temperament. It is of great benefit to the parent when he realizes that it is natural for his child to have a desire for evil. The child is not just being obstinate and uncooperative but is following that natural desire to learn more about and to experience *evil*. There is a conflict going on within him because he has not yet been quickened or alerted to spiritual values.

He is born with very selfish desires and thinks only of his own wants. When denied his wants, he reacts with rage and fits of anger. Can you see what a teenager or an adult would be like if left to those natural ego-centered desires? The parent who understands these natural tendencies will be more intent in leading his child to know Christ and in teaching him to abhor evil and desire the good in life.

Too few parents seem to comprehend the tremendous impact

WHAT IT TAKES TO GROW A CHILD

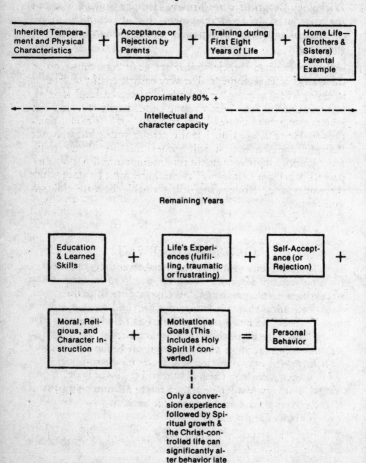

First Eight Years of Life

| Inherited Tempera-ment and Physical Characteristics | + | Acceptance or Rejection by Parents | + | Training during First Eight Years of Life | + | Home Life— (Brothers & Sisters) Parental Example |

Approximately 80% +

Intellectual and character capacity

Remaining Years

| Education & Learned Skills | + | Life's Experi-ences (fulfil-ling, traumatic or frustrating) | + | Self-Accept-ance (or Rejection) | + |

| Moral, Reli-gious, and Character instruction | + | Motivational Goals (This includes Holy Spirit if con-verted) | = | Personal Behavior |

Only a conver-sion experience followed by Spi-ritual growth & the Christ-con-trolled life can significantly al-ter behavior late in life.

their teaching or negligence has during the first eight years of their children's lives. The chart on page 4 is used by my husband in one of the courses he teaches in the Biblical Psychology Department at Christian Heritage College. It shows the areas in a child's development that affects 80% of his intellectual and character capacities already determined by the age of eight.

Parents need to conscientiously set goals for themselves in these areas of development. The very earliest sparks of interest in doing good need to be nurtured, protected, and trained. How beautiful it is to hear a young child, barely able to put a sentence together, quote "God is love," or "We love Him because He first loved us." If this tender young plant is not nurtured and watered, it will wither and die. There is no waiting until a more convenient time. Children will not wait for parents' schedules to improve. The training must be done while they are young, tender, and still trainable because children won't wait.

CHILDREN WON'T WAIT

There is a time to anticipate the baby's coming, a time
   to consult a doctor;
A time to plan a diet and exercise, a time to gather a
   layette.
There is a time to wonder at the ways of God, knowing
   this is the destiny for which I was crafted;
A time to dream of what this child may become,
A time to pray that God will teach me how to train
   this child which I bear.
A time to prepare myself that I might nurture his soul.
But soon there comes the time for birth,
For babies won't wait.

There is a time for night feedings, and colic and
   formulas.
There is a time for rocking and a time for walking the
   floor,

A time for patience and self-sacrifice,

A time to show him that his new world is a world of love and goodness and dependability.

There is a time to ponder what he is—not a pet nor toy, but a person, an individual—a soul made in God's image.

There is a time to consider my stewardship. I cannot possess him.

He is not mine. I have been chosen to care for him, to love him, to enjoy him, to nurture him, and to answer to God.

I resolve to do my best for him,

For babies don't wait.

There is a time to hold him close and tell him the sweetest story ever told;

A time to show him God in earth and sky and flower, to teach him to wonder and reverence.

There is a time to leave the dishes, to swing him in the park.

To run a race, to draw a picture, to catch a butterfly, to give him happy comradeship.

There is a time to point the way, to teach his infant lips to pray,

To teach his heart to love God's Word, to love God's day.

For children don't wait.

There is a time to sing instead of grumble, to smile instead of frown,

To kiss away the tears and laugh at broken dishes.

A time to share with him my best in attitudes—a love of life, a love of God, a love of family.

There is a time to answer his questions, all his questions,

Because there may come a time when he will not want my answers.

There is a time to teach him so patiently to obey, to

put his toys away.
There is a time to teach him the beauty of duty, the habit of Bible study, the joy of worship at home, the peace of prayer.
For children don't wait.

There is a time to watch him bravely go to school, to miss him underfoot,
And to know that other minds have his attention, but that I will be there to answer his call when he comes home,
And listen eagerly to the story of his day.
There is a time to teach him independence, responsibility, self-reliance,
To be firm but friendly, to discipline with love,
For soon, so soon, there will be a time to let him go, the apron strings untied,
For children won't wait.

There is a time to treasure every fleeting minute of his childhood.
Just eighteen precious years to inspire and train him.
I will not exchange this birthright for a mess of pottage called social position, or business or professional reputation, or a pay check.
An hour of concern today may save years of heartache tomorrow,
The house will wait, the dishes will wait, the new room can wait,
But children don't wait.

There will be a time when there will be no slamming of doors, no toys on the stairs, no childhood quarrels, no fingerprints on the wallpaper.
Then may I look back with joy and not regret.
There will be a time to concentrate on service outside my home,
On visiting the sick, the bereaved, the discouraged, the untaught;

To give myself to the "least of these."

There will be a time to look back and know that these
    years of motherhood were not wasted.

I pray there will be a time to see him an upright and
    honest man, loving God and serving all.

God, give me wisdom to see that today is my day with
    my children.

That there is no unimportant moment in their lives.

May I know that no other career is so precious,

No other work so rewarding,

No other task so urgent.

May I not defer it nor neglect it,

But by thy Spirit accept it gladly, joyously, and by thy
    grace realize

That the time is short and my time is now,

For children won't wait!

—Helen M. Young

(Used by permission)

2

It Helps To
Know Your Child

The young family had just arrived at Grandma's house. She welcomed them by taking the darling six-week-old baby in her arms to love and admire. After several moments of being ignored and feeling left out, the little four-year-old tugged at Grandma's skirt and said hesitantly, "Grandma, I'm here!"

I am sure most grandmas would not consciously do such a thing, but, unfortunately, there are many children who are feeling left out because no one takes the time to see them for who they really are. The four-year-old needs to be known for himself and wants the attention and affection equal to what is given the new baby. Even though youngsters may be different sexes and completely different temperaments, their need to be "known" will be similar.

Each child will undoubtedly be a different temperament than his brothers and sisters. The genes that aid in determining the temperaments are contributed from the two parents, four grandparents, and perhaps even a third generation.

After the birth of our first child, a gynecologist assured us that she was absolutely unique. He said that if we had twenty children, they would each be completely different with varying personalities and temperaments. And that is true. Each of our four children were very different, even though they stemmed from the same two parents and the same four grandparents. By the time they had turned two years old, we had already begun to see absolute differences and recognized a unique originality in each child.

Linda was our firstborn. She entered the world with a lovely, cheerful disposition. Since she was a curious child and very active, our quiet little household became a rumpus room of activity. After two years of living, it was easy to detect that she was a natural leader as she directed her dolls and stuffed animals into obedience. Her ability to express herself with words developed at an early age and she used it often. She responded very well to correction and discipline and had a sensitive heart for spiritual things. As we got to know her better, we began to appreciate her thoughtful concern for the welfare of others, her leadership ability, and her keen sense for right and wrong. If we had not taken the time to really know her, these strengths could have been overlooked and never encouraged and developed. Linda was truly a delightful child to raise.

After two years Larry came along. He seemed to slip quietly into our family with not too much fanfare. Since he was quiet-natured and easily contented, he could amuse himself for long periods of time. And, of course, he had a sister to help entertain him. He did not often assert himself but was content to go along with his sister's wishes. At the age of two he would sit and study his playthings, seeming to be in deep thought as to how to create new ways of playing with old toys. His pensive moments would be interspersed with mischievousness, making him a lovable and interesting little package. He was a little more difficult to get to know because of his quietness and lack of expression. How important it was for his proper development that we took the time to study and know him. Many fine qualities would have been overlooked and passed by. Inside the quiet child is often a reservoir of talents that need to be let loose and properly directed.

Lee arrived three years after Larry. His entrance into the world was similar to that of an explosion. This boy was an adorable child, and loving him was like loving both a kitten and a lion at the same time. He could purr and roar with one breath. His complexity was a challenge to us, but still he entwined himself around our heartstrings with his tender, loving ways. Before his second birthday we had already noticed two distinct characteristics: One was his strong will and unending determination, and the second was a gifted mind which God had given him. Taking the time to know Lee probably made the difference of his becoming a well-adjusted young man rather than a rebellious heartbreak to his parents. As we got to recognize and know his mood changes, we were better able to help him by our own understanding attitudes. He tested our patience and our discipline, but he responded with a sensitive spirit and provided a lovable and challenging experience for us as parents.

Four years later our fourth child arrived in the form of a little girl named Lori. She was a happy, giggly, and bubbly baby. Her charisma was a beautiful blend with the temperaments of the other three. When conflicts would arise between the children, she was the peacemaker who would give in to restore tranquility and harmony. Her desire to please was so strong that she was rarely disobedient; on the few occasions when she was, there was little need for stern discipline. A disapproving look from Mom or Dad was about all that was necessary. Her first two years of living revealed that the world was her stage and she was the star. In many ways it has been her cheerful approach to life that has woven the threads of warmth and close fellowship throughout our family. It was not too difficult to really know Lori because she was open and candid about everything. We had to learn quickly that, because of her active involvement with life, it was necessary for us to be able to rise and fall with her joys and sorrows.

All four children have made a definite impact on our lives, and they were loved and adored equally by us. But how different they were! Each one contributed individual talents and assets in making the family unity that we now enjoy. The varying joys and sorrows they created taught us to learn to cope with each child according to his own temperament. A super-sensitive child cannot be dealt with in the same way as the child who is bull-headed and strong-willed. Nor can the fearful child be treated in the same way as the bold, aggressive child.

To assist in the proper development and training of children, it is of great importance that during each child's early years the parents learn his temperament characteristics. The heart and center of the parent-child relationship is knowing and understanding each child.

3

Why Your Kids
Act The Way They Do

"I don't understand why Johnny acts like he does. He sure doesn't get it from his father or me!" These were the exact words of a frustrated mother who could not understand why her Johnny acted like he did. It would have helped if she had realized that he acted as he did because of the combinations of genes received from his parents and perhaps even his grandparents. The influence of these six or more different people contribute to the temperament of one child. Is it any wonder some children resemble their parents, others are more like their grandparents, while still others do not resemble either because they are a blend of several combinations of people?

My husband's two books, *Spirit-Controlled Temperament* and *Transformed Temperaments* (Tyndale House Publishers), give a very detailed presentation of the four basic temperaments. This study is continued and directed toward women in my last book, *Spirit-Controlled Woman*, (Harvest House Publishers). Then the latest book on this subject written by my husband is entitled, *Understanding the Male Temperament* (Fleming H. Revell). I would suggest that you refer to these writings for a complete study of the temperaments. However, in the pages that follow, I will discuss immature temperament traits as observed in children.

In preparation for writing this book I have had many rap sessions with mothers whose children were of various temperaments and ages. My two married daughters, Linda and Kathy, encouraged me in helping me observe their children and in planning sessions for me with many of their friends.

One primary observation we have all made is that by the time a child is two years old, he has begun to fit into a temperament category. Please remember that no one is a single temperament. We are unique combinations of at least two and occasionally three temperaments. We will be discussing the child's immature characteristics, which are, nonetheless, the beginning resemblance of what he will become. Because we are dealing with immaturity, the child will not be locked into absolute temperament traits. At different stages of growth and development, he will react with some degree of variance. Inhibitions may cause him to alter and subdue some of his basic traits, and environment can be a great influence on him while he is finding himself. On the other hand, he may be affected by new motivations that will result in a temporary change of pattern.

His ways are unstable during these formative years; however, the majority of the time he will resemble the temperament he is becoming. Let us take a look at the childish traits of the four basic temperaments: Sanguine, Choleric, Melancholic and Phlegmatic.

Sammy and Suzy Sanguine

The little sanguine can be easily recognized by his friendly and steady talkativeness. Nobody is a stranger—everyone is his best friend. Even before he learns to talk he can say so much with his cheerful disposition and devilish personality. His winning smile keeps him from many a scolding, and he may try to get through life by being Mr. Friendly. He is the child that sits on the seat of a grocery basket and rides through the grocery store asking everyone what their name is and where they live. This temperament is the one who will stand out in a group of children by being the loudest and the most boisterous. He has a short interest span and will restlessly flit from stacking blocks to climbing on chairs, flipping the TV switches, or any other mischievous thing his mind happens to think of. The world is his stage and he will clown or show-off to be the center of attention. In little children we think this to be cute, but when they reach the junior age, it seems disgusting. Yet they are the same temperament with the same traits but with bigger bodies. Usually, Sammy is a mimic and you will see him acting like people he has been around. All children are pretenders, but the sanguine will be able to pretend and get over it—a very normal and healthy characteristic.

One of our grandchildren is a lovable sanguine. He has been the cause of some very tense moments for his grandmother. Sanguines are usually daredevils, climbers, act-now-and-think-later people. This little man was all of that. One day at my home I walked into the entry to see him climbing on the outside edge of a stair railing that had a drop of about twelve feet to a hard tile surface below. His little hands were hanging tightly to the railing while his toes were barely able to fit on the small area outside the railing. Just as he took his last step to the highest ledge, he turned to me with a winning smile. He was not yet two and was not talking much, but if he had been able, he probably would have said, "Hi, Grandma, look what I've done!" There was no fear at that moment, (except in *my* heart), just smiles and joy at his accomplishment. The fear came when I told him he had to come down, and he could only get down the same way he got up. He cried every step down as I encouraged him and insisted he keep coming. Sanguines are very prone to act on impulse and then think later. I wish that I could say he learned his lesson and never tried it again. Unfortunately, he had to try it several times before he learned that I meant what I said about staying off the railing.

One observation I have made is that this temperament seems to be eager to please. The little sanguines in my life seem very willing to say "please" and "thank you." They fully intend to be obedient and please, but they get swept away with curiosity or a change of environment. Although many times he may seem to be premeditatedly disobedient, he actually is just forgetting the past and engulfed in the present moment. He easily forgets the past punishments and does not consider the problems his disobedience may present him.

Even when punished severely, he quickly changes his mood and may be heard singing or whistling only moments later. Two little children were spanked for disobeying and then sent to their individual rooms until they finished crying. The choleric child must have stayed there for fifteen or twenty minutes, all the time screaming and complaining loudly. The little sanguine was over his sadness in thirty seconds and dashed outside to play. Two minutes later he was on his swing set sailing high into the sky and singing at the top of his lungs, "Jesus loves me, this I know." Even after the twenty minutes, when the choleric came out of her room she was anything but happy. She drooped around and complained for at least an hour.

A sanguine has a difficult time playing alone. He is so people oriented that it is very important for him to have brothers, sisters, or neighbors to play with. He loves to share himself and his possessions to gain new friends. His loving nature can change to immediate anger when something crosses him. The explosion may resemble a volcano erupting, but he will readily apologize and beg for forgiveness. He is the little child on the playground that cries, "I'm sorry, I didn't mean to." His emotions are a combination of highs and lows shown by his laughter that is quickly changed to tears, and vice versa.

Because of his quick changing moods, he can readily adjust to disappointments and make the best of the situation. I watched a sanguine teen-age girl go through a series of disappointments in her high school years that would have finished off any melancholic. After each disappointment she hit an emotional low but came out of every experience with a beautiful, rejoicing spirit. She had parents that would not allow her to engage in self-pity but encouraged her to look for the things that she could be thankful for. The danger for this temperament is that after a discouragement he may drift into a pattern of feeling sorry for himself and thus remain in a depressed state.

The sanguine is rarely a good student because of his restlessness. He probably has the capabilities but his undisciplined and weak-willed nature will hinder his settling down to good study habits. He can overcome this if he is taught to discipline himself in all areas of life and to allow the Holy Spirit to make use of his great potential.

This carefree, happy-go-lucky temperament will be difficult to recognize when he does not have the security of a loving and stable home. He needs to be loved and accepted by others, particularly his family. When his parents are quarrelsome and unhappy, then he reflects that spirit by becoming sullen and withdrawn. How important it is for the proper development of all temperaments to be raised in a loving and secure home!

The sanguine will be responsive to spiritual things. He has a compassionate heart and responds to those who love him. When he hears that God loved him and that Jesus died for him, his tender sanguine heart will respond readily. He may walk in and out of fellowship with Christ because he is a follower without strong convictions, but he is usually willing to repent and start over again. Most sanguine children who are exposed to the gospel message receive Christ at an early age. They need careful guidelines to direct them as they walk through their youthful years.

Chucky and Cindy Choleric

Probably one of the earliest temperaments to discern in children is the choleric. By two years of age he will have developed an independent spirit and will attempt to do things for himself that other children would not try until much later. This could include anything from feeding himself, tying his own shoes, to riding a bicycle. The choleric child is quite self-sufficient and rather insistent in climbing out of a stroller or walking through the shopping center unassisted. Unlike the phlegmatic, who quietly and stubbornly will disobey and do his own thing, the choleric will loudly and angrily proclaim his disapproval and then proceed to show you. He is easily recognized by his strong will and determined spirit. This strong will need not be a hindrance to the spiritual growth of the child if the parent can break that will at an early age.

Suzanna Wesley, the mother of nineteen, said, "The self-willed child must be broken and brought into subjection before he reaches two years of age." She must have found the key that works because two of her sons shook the continents of Great Britain and North America with their ministry for God.

It is the will that must be broken and not the spirit of the choleric. The young person who has a strong will that is totally submitted to God will be greatly helped by this strength of character to stand against the temptations of that age. He has the potential to be a leader of great influence rather than a follower.

The young choleric, like the mature one, will be an active person and a strong leader. Our choleric daughter was a dominant leader among the neighborhood children. Some were older, yet she was not affected by their age. She could organize and lead the sandbox activity, the jump rope competition, or the family schedule for doing dishes. It was her natural gift that God had built into her. Had she not submitted her dominant spirit to the Lord to control and use for His glory, she could have turned into an abusive person and a poor marriage partner. Today this young woman still has the gift of leadership, but she is a beautiful example of a Spirit-controlled wife who is submissive both to God and to her husband. The Lord has sharpened this gift in her but has smoothed off the rough edges, and He continues to put her in areas of leadership where she can be effective and pleasing to God. He wants her to use the gifts of her temperament; however, they must be controlled by the Holy Spirit.

One trait of this temperament that frequently surfaces is blunt, sarcastic speech. Because the choleric is self-confident and not always concerned about pleasing people, he will speak what he thinks, even though it may be cutting or offensive. Little children are naturally honest and straightforward because they are uninhibited; however, the choleric child is not only honest but almost brutal. He will test you to see how far you will let him go. One of our grandchildren tested my authority one day by disobeying and announcing to me, "You are not my mother and I don't have to mind you!" Now I didn't take this personally nor feel offended. I knew that this little choleric was simply testing me, and I needed to prove to her that she did have to mind me when she was left in my care. I believe that I have succeeded because she now respects my authority and we have a loving relationship together. It took a confrontation and a breaking of her will to accomplish this.

When two choleric children play together, you can be sure there will be conflict almost immediately. Since this temperament has to be the boss of the group, and there is usually room for only one, they tend to gravitate to the other temperaments whom they can dominate.

One day while entertaining my grandchildren during the Christmas holidays, I observed how different temperaments responded to a similar situation. Our Christmas tree had a special hanging ornament that was of sentimental value, and I did not want the children playing with it. When I realized it was within their reach and all three of them were attracted to it, I moved it higher on the tree and offered them a less vaulable object to play with. The sanguine child seemed equally as interested in the new object and could not have cared less about the valuable one. The phlegmatic studied it carefully and then stood back to see what the other children were going to do. Not the choleric! That child resounded loudly that she didn't like the substitute ornament and wanted the first one. I explained that this was a special one that was to be looked at but not touched and the second ornament was one they could handle and admire. In a few moments this determined child had pushed a chair up to the tree, and I caught her just as her hand was about to grasp the ornament. After dealing with the situation and the disobedience, I removed the temptation and placed the ornament on a high shelf in the closet until the children had left. Much later I entered the room to find that this same child had dragged a chair across the room and was hanging by her fingertips trying to reach the forbidden ornament. Such determination becomes an admirable characteristic only when it can be submitted to authority and directed toward goals that are productive and beneficial.

The choleric child needs to have definite areas of responsibility and leadership. It is very necessary for him to develop this natural born characteristic under the watchful eye and loving direction of his parents. The degree of responsibility should increase with the age and development of the child. The choleric has an active mind and it can best be controlled and directed by putting him in charge of responsible areas. This temperament thrives on activity that is productive. I have seen a teenage choleric very successfully take the full responsibility and leadership of a high school banquet. He accepted the challenge and rose to the occasion. With committees selected and organized, ne proceeded to move at top speed. Unfortunately, the committees were not all cholerics and did not have the same drive and determination that he did. The other temperaments had difficulty working with this leader because he had a tendency to be a hard driver and unreasonable with his demands. When the others fell short, the young choleric strongly reprimanded them and expressed his feelings regarding their inadequacy, then picked up their unfinished load and completed the project himself. However, in spite of how he accomplished his goal, the end result was very successful. What he needed to learn was how to lead and motivate other temperaments to carry their share of the load. This could only come from experience and maturity.

The choleric child should be led to the Lord by the time he is twelve years old or the chances of a later decision for Christ become very slim. He is the most responsive to spiritual things before that time. This is probably because of his natural characteristic to be self-confident and self-sufficient. After his junior years, his confidence grows with maturity and he rarely feels the need of a Heavenly Father. His natural characteristic is not to be a leaner, and it becomes difficult for him to depend on the Holy Spirit for help and guidance. His motto is, "I can do it myself."

Milty and Molly Melancholy

This temperament can be the most gifted and have the deepest depression all wrapped up in one little package. God has endowed him with a brilliant mind and the ability to be a creative, deep thinker. His sensitive, artistic nature is often affected by his attitude towards others or what he thinks their attitudes toward him might be. It is easy for him to have his feelings hurt and to feel inferior, believing that others do not like him. Even though he may possess the greatest talents of any of the temperaments, he suffers under the delusion of an inferiority complex. Parents of a melancholic child should be especially considerate of this problem. Because of his sensitive nature and his tendency toward perfection, he cannot handle criticism and will sink deeper into an inferior state.

A little two-year-old is capable of showing his temperament traits by switching from one mood to another without too much cause. The extremity of his mood swings will be determined by his secondary temperament, which will be discussed in the next chapter. He can sit sullen and quiet, enjoying his loneliness, and then later become outgoing, aggressive, and an actor much like a sanguine.

It is possible that he will learn to escape reality by living in a make-believe, fantasy world. The wise parents will continually bring him back to face the reality and any consequences that accompany it. When little Johnny repeatedly says, "I didn't do it—Tommy did," and Tommy is an imaginary friend, then Johnny needs to learn that he cannot hide behind Tommy. He needs to face the reality of confessing, "I did it." Too many Johnnys have grown up to continually blame others for their mistakes or disobedience instead of admitting their own wrong doing, confessing it, and facing the consequences.

This child has such great potential, but he needs so much help and understanding! When left to his own ways he will no doubt grow up to become a gloomy, pessimistic, self-pitying individual. Fortunately, God gave these children parents to teach them how to have joy and thankfulness instead of gloom, a wholesome, positive attitude instead of a negative attitude, and a spirit of praise instead of self-pity.

We watched a melancholic junior boy, who had most of the weaknesses of this temperament, develop into a complainer with a critical spirit. One day his parents realized something had to be done so they prayerfully approached him and openly discussed it. It was their decision, in an effort to help him, that they would not approve of him speaking negatively or critically again. When he did, it would be brought to his attention and he would have to replace it with a positive and thankful statement. They wanted him to learn to be silent if he could not say something good and praiseworthy about a subject. It has been interesting to watch this boy after about eight or ten years. He has a new spirit and seems much happier with himself because of it.

A friend of mine received several letters from her daughter who was away for a few weeks over the summer. She shared the letters with me; they were filled with nothing but problems she had been faced with and some real disappointments. I concluded that the girl was having a terrible time and that every possible difficulty was happening to her. When she returned we were able to spend some time together, and I commented how sorry I was that the experience had been such a disastrous one. She was stunned by my reaction and quickly informed me that she had had the time of her life. In her letters she had dwelt on just the problems and never mentioned the great time she was having.

Negativism is a habit pattern we easily slip into, and it is best broken when we are still young and pliable and able to change.

Even though the melancholic is the most gifted, he will be the last one to recognize it. He has a poor self-image and entertains many feelings of failure and inability. Parents should start when he is very young to help him see what God has given him in talents and abilities and then learn to thank God for them.

This child sets very high goals for himself, and when they are not reached, he gets very depressed. When he does not receive an ''A'' on the test paper, he is sure he is failing the course and becomes very discouraged. If the model airplane that he is building does not look better than the one on the box lid, he is sure he is a failure. When the melancholic girl's home-baked cookies do not taste just like Mother's, she is certain she will never be able to bake. He is overly conscientious and everything has to be nearly perfect. This tendency leads him to produce very excellent term papers or reports that are both attractive and well written.

My daughter went through school with a lovely melancholic girl friend. This girl had many of the strengths of her temperament, and because of her spiritual growth, the weaknesses were not too pronounced. These girls were very best of friends through the elementary grades, junior high, and high school. Other girl friends would come and go with each passing year, but these two remained fast, loyal friends. I watched while their friendship was tested time and time again, and even though it seemed rocky for awhile, they would emerge faithful, loyal friends. One of the admirable characteristics of the melancholic is that he is such a faithful friend. Even today when the girls are separated by two thousand miles because they are attending different colleges, the mail service between these two friends is kept busy. We feel fortunate that our daughter has such a beautiful and loyal friend!

The melancholic young person may be the last one in the family to marry—regardless whether he is male or female. He will have difficulty finding someone to meet up to his perfectionist and idealistic standards for a life partner. Some have been known to back out of the wedding at the last moment because they got cold feet when they realized that their new partner was not perfect. It is far better that he change his mind before the wedding than after, but sometimes it has just been the fear of making such a weighty decision that keeps him from the marriage altar.

After discussing melancholic children with many different mothers, I have drawn one strong conclusion: Parents of melancholic children rarely agree on how to raise them. Many have expressed that the most severe clashes in their marriage regarding raising children were how to discipline their melancholic child.

One mother told me that, after twenty-two years of a good, solid marriage, she and her husband developed a critical and antagonistic spirit toward one another over their differences regarding their melancholic child. She accused him of being too harsh and insensitive toward this tender child, and he felt that she was ruining the child by being over-protective. Every time he attempted to discipline the child, he felt that she was disapproving; and, according to her story, she probably was.

In other instances it has been the mother who was thought to be overly harsh and the father who was the protector. It is most likely the parent who has the more extrovert temperament who will be accused of being hard and insensitive to the melancholic. The introvert will tend to draw him under a protective wing.

This temperament has the potential in his strengths to be outstanding with his gifts and creativity and excel among his peers. But he also has the capability in his weaknesses to sink below his companions with his strong feelings of inferiority and pessimism. From this we can conclude that the melancholic is rarely an average child because he has the greatest strengths and the most devastating weaknesses.

Peter and Polly Phlegmatic

The most enjoyable child to raise may be the one who has a predominantly phlegmatic temperament, only because he is naturally quiet, easygoing, and calm. This baby is usually the contented one and will be happy just lying in the crib looking at the four corners of the ceiling. Because he is not demanding of a mother's time and attention, she may be guilty of taking advantage of his calmness and not spending the time to cuddle and play with him that he needs.

As he grows from infancy to young childhood, he may be slow at learning to talk, not because he lacks intelligence, but because he is not too expressive anyway and is just being a spectator of life. This is especially true if he thinks someone else will do the talking for him. His motto is, "Why overexert myself?"

I recently asked my little phlegmatic grandson what his dog's name was. By the time he had his lips in position to answer, my choleric granddaughter had already responded for him and was off to handle another situation.

He is usually a slow eater and may enjoy just rearranging the food on his plate. Unlike the sanguine who lives to eat (if he can be silent long enough), the phlegmatic may not put that much importance on eating unless it is a favorite food that he really enjoys.

One parent told me of her phlegmatic child who was slowly enjoying his dinner. The dessert had been set at each plate on the table at the beginning of the meal. The little phlegmatic had diddle-daddled along through the whole meal and, as usual, was the last one at the table eating. He finished his meal and, thinking he was through, left the table. It was not until the next day that he remembered he had not eaten his dessert, but it had not been left on the table. His sanguine brother confessed that he had taken the dessert when his brother was not looking and, after waiting so long for him to notice it was gone, finally decided to eat it himself. That is enough to make a slow "phleg" eat like a hungry sanguine!

Because this temperament is an introvert, his weaknesses may not show too readily, particularly when he is young. Since his greatest problem is a lack of motivation, he can skirt around this during his younger years. Oh yes, you will notice his attempts to ignore your instructions to put away his toys, to hang up his pajamas, or to finish doing the dishes.

Another weakness the phlegmatic is bothered with is his stinginess or selfishness. Most young children have a problem with sharing their belongings with other children, but the phlegmatic tends not to outgrow this. As a young child, when other temperaments are beginning to share and be generous, he can be seen gathering his things under his wings for protection and control.

I was a guest in a certain home where there were three children, ages 3, 4, and 6. Other friends, who had two more children around the same ages as my friend's, were expected to arrive. The three children were happily playing together with a building set on the family room floor when the doorbell rang. The parents announced that the friends had arrived with the two other children. I observed the three-year-old sanguine gather as many toys in her two hands as she could hold and rush to the door to share them with the visiting children. Meanwhile the four-year-old phlegmatic began to scoop the remaining toys around him so he could begin stuffing them into his pockets and under his sweat shirt. By the time the guests had entered the room, he was standing there with pockets bulging, sweat shirt sagging, and looking very much like an overstuffed teddy bear. He was not about to share with these intruders.

The phlegmatic child will be the easiest of the temperaments to take into a restaurant for a meal. Even though he may not engage in eating too well, he will entertain himself by watching the activity going on around him. The same is true when taking him into a church service. All churches do not have nurseries for the youngsters. Recently I sat in the back during a service and noticed two young children sitting with their parents in front of me. One child, who was obviously choleric and sanguine, had her parents sitting on the edge of the pew while she demanded their full attention during the service. Finally, in desperation, the mother picked up the child and walked out the door. Just as she passed by, I caught a sparkling gleam in the child's eye that said loud and clear, "Finally, she's taking me out!" On the same pew sat another couple with a child about the same age and even the same sex. This little girl was sitting on her daddy's lap deeply engrossed in a baby's hairbrush. She was carefully examining every bristle on the brush and then would gently stroke her hair from every angle. Her parents were listening intently to the sermon and paid little attention to the child. Why the vast difference? One was definitely a quiet, calm phlegmatic while the other was an active, determined choleric.

One of the greatest joys a phlegmatic can have is successfully teasing. Teasing can be a pleasant pastime or it can be his way of getting back at a person who annoys him. His strategy is to tease long enough so that the person who has annoyed him will eventually blow up or become unglued. They also enjoy teasing just for the sake of teasing. Our son knew that our daughter scared easily. Nothing delighted him more than to slip quietly into the laundry room where his sister would not hear him because of the noise from the washer and dryer. He would get right behind her and then give off a loud yell. She would nearly jump out of her skin and many times broke into tears just from fright. They laugh about it today, but years ago his teasing was a real trauma in our daughter's life.

As this temperament grows into the teen years, he may become uninvolved with his peer group and activities that would benefit him socially and spiritually. He needs to be encouraged to be a participant and not just a spectator. He will have much to offer society but will probably need a gentle push to get involved. It is very important that he learn responsibility during his growing years so that he can gain his freedom when he reaches adulthood.

4

Twelve Blends Of Children's Temperaments

After reading Chapter Three you may find it somewhat difficult to identify your children's temperaments. This is because no one exactly fits the description of one temperament only; we are all a blend of at least two. For that reason, this chapter will discuss the twelve most common blends of the temperaments. Most parents find it easier to identify their children as one of the twelve blends than as one of the four basic temperaments.

Certainly all blends are not the same proportion. A child who is 75% sanguine and 25% choleric (we call him "SanChlor") will be quite different from the child who is 80% choleric and 20% sanguine ("ChlorSan"). In breaking down the temperaments on the following pages, I have used the proportions of 60% for the primary temperament and 40% for the secondary. In a single chapter I could not possibly list all the potential combinations of percentages within the twelve blends of temperaments, but a brief discussion of the 60-40% combinations will provide some indication of the basic trends. This additional information should enable you to make any further breakdown of the proportions for yourself.

SanChlor

Since both of these temperaments are outgoing by themselves, they become a very strong extrovert when blended. The enthusiasm of the sanguine combined with the drive and character of the choleric creates a more productive person than one who is totally sanguine. The influence of the choleric gives him a bit more determination than he would normally have. Whatever the SanChlor person does, he must have activity and excitement. If there is none, he will persist until he gets it going.

He loves sports but must be a participant, not an observer. If he isn't fortunate enough to be on the team, he will certainly be the loudest spectator in the stand. The girl who cannot play in a fellow's sport will be involved as a cheerleader, in a drill team, flag corps, or any other activity where she can enter with her bundle of enthusiasm.

The SanChlor is extremely talkative and usually says and tells more than he ought—not only about himself but sometimes about his parents or friends. By his persistent talking he usually reveals his weak points and would be better off to say less. In school he will tell all that happens at home. Is it any wonder that the first time parents meet his school teacher, she looks at them like they might have two heads? He usually speaks before he thinks, and, regardless of the subject, he speaks as an authority. This uninhibited child has a giant ego; therefore, he does not wear well over a long period of time with members of his peer group. If he senses the other children resisting him, he will come on stronger, causing them to resist him even more. He is either the lovable, fun-loving member in his group, or, when he feels threatened, he will be the obnoxious bore.

Anger is one of the major problems with which the SanChlor has to cope. When he has been crossed, his anger comes to the top immediately and he explodes all over everyone. It is easy to tell when he is being disrespectful—his mouth gives him away.

Although the SanChlor repents easily, he needs to be taught that he cannot defy his parents one minute to "get it off his chest," then apologize quickly the next minute to avoid the deserved punishment. He is a natural "con artist" who can go from anger to tears of repentance within four seconds. He needs to learn that a quick and easy repentance is not the same as a positive change in behavior.

When punishment is needed for the SanChlors, you will find that sitting in their room is often more effective than spanking. Because they are so restless, they would much rather get spanked quickly to get it over with so they can be on their way out the door.

The parents of the SanChlor need to help the child face his own wrong deeds and to teach him to take full responsibility for his mistakes and sins. He needs to learn that consideration for others must come before his own interests or goals and that circumstances in life are not always going to center around him. His anger usually stems from not getting his own way and can best be helped by not giving in to him or catering to his temper fits. From earliest childhood his parents need to help him develop habits of consistency, following through, and self-discipline. Otherwise, he will dissipate his many natural capabilities as he grows up.

Probably his greatest need is learning to finish what he starts. The sanguine has the ability to start more things than he could ever finish. Having a portion of choleric helps the SanChlor in this area; however, he still needs to avoid taking on more than he can complete. Many a sanguine gets excited about Boy Scouts just long enough to get his uniform, and then when he has to work for merit badges, he loses interest. Training in this discipline should begin at an early age. When the young child gets out a box of toys, he should not be permitted to leave them to play with something else before picking them up and putting them away. The parent will probably have to assist in this during the early years, but the child should at least be hovering over the box while it is being done. Far more important than his helping to keep the house in order is your task of building character in the child and developing his much needed art of self-discipline.

SanMel

The SanMel is highly emotional and fluctuates drastically between a flood of tears and hysterical laughter. He will both laugh and weep with his friends, depending upon the situation. In fact, he can be weeping one minute and then, for no reason at all, begin laughing at himself, or vice versa. These children genuinely feel the hurt of others; they show real sorrow at the death of a pet or any animal.

They are very apt to be involved in acting, public speaking, or music. Because they are people oriented, they will most likely participate in activities that give them an audience. One little SanMel girl was so desirous to perform that she developed a stage and props in the garage for her weekly performances. Sanguine children are born actors looking for a stage on which to perform.

Both sanguines and melancholics are dreamers, and as long as the sanguine force predominates, his dreams will be positive, in full color, and with stereophonic sound. But when the melancholic influence suggests a negative train of thought, his dreams return to black and white and begin to tumble; he starts to feel that he isn't capable of doing anything well and his self-image suffers. His moods may vary from exuberant highs to depressing lows.

The sanguine has a problem with temper and the melancholic with fear; therefore, the SanMel is usually confronted with both fear and temper problems. This produces insecurity and he needs to be surrounded by people who love him and accept him as he is. It is so important to him to be well thought of by others. He needs to be reassured of parental love and approval often.

This temperament has an aesthetic nature and should be exposed to music lessons at a young age. Many of these children have started lessons and then talked their parents into letting them stop after a short while, only to regret it when they become older. Of all the temperament blends, SanMel is most apt to be an uninhibited performer with a natural "ear" for music. Encouragement and discipline to keep up his lessons while young will provide him both with opportunities to help others and to serve the Lord later in life and with training in the development of self-discipline. The SanMel, who often has many capabilities and talents, may never reach his potential because his parents failed to teach him the importance of self-discipline needed to reach a goal. He needs to work at becoming an achiever.

These children are prone to be fantastic fibbers. They are not satisfied with telling little "white lies." When they "fib" the stories are usually so outlandish they are obviously not the truth. Like the little boy who told his mother that he didn't break the window when, in fact, he was the only one outside and had a bat in his hand. He also has the ability to be a "snow artist" and talk his way out of anything, especially in the face of punishment. This is the child who nervously tries to talk himself out of a spanking just before the paddle comes down on the designated place; he is quite capable at making a parent feel guilty for administering the spanking he earned.

The SanMel child will be socially conscious and an activist. He will be well-liked by friends and less obnoxious than the SanChlor. However, he is more of a perfectionist than the SanChlor and may alienate others by his verbal criticism of them. He needs to develop an understanding of and compassion for less capable people than himself. He often has a quick, retentive mind that needs to be disciplined to learning during his early years.

When this child has been taught proper self-discipline, he can become a real disciple for Jesus Christ because he has a genuine sensitivity toward spiritual things that usually reveals itself early in a Christian home. He may best excel in the fields of social science, math, science, or music, if he has learned to be an achiever and not a quitter.

SanPhleg

The most enjoyable children to raise can be the SanPhlegs when they aren't permitted to indulge their weaknesses. They are lovable, affectionate, happy little busybodies that rarely cause trouble. Like other sanguines, they want what they want—right now—but they don't get quite as upset if they can't have it. Their interest span is extremely short-lived, and they are easily distracted by sounds or movement, particularly if it suggests people or activity. They are animal lovers and usually sleep with their pets. One two-year-old SanPhleg who saw tears running down the face of a family friend, climbed up in her lap and said, "Aunt Shirley, let me kiss your tears away," and then proceeded to try. They just naturally love people of any age.

The SanPhleg combines the uninhibited extroversion of the sanguine and the witty good humor of the phlegmatic, so they are usually very funny and delight in making others laugh. One salesman said after fitting a suit on a five-year-old, "I'll bet you get a lot of laughs out of this kid." And usually you do if you give him lots of love. Although he is a lovable type, the SanPhleg is not perfect. Despite his natural charm and people-loving ways, the sanguine lack of discipline and the phlegmatic lack of motivation may frequently prove to be his undoing in life. If you have one of these fun-loving children, don't let his charisma and "big liquid eyes" blind you to the need to start teaching him early that he cannot be a quitter.

No one can leave his room in a greater disaster than the SanPhleg. One such teenager's father came in to awaken her one morning and found that the party clothes she had worn the night before were lying right where she had stepped out of them. In rage, he jerked her closet open to find thirty-eight items of clothing lying on the floor. Of all children, they are the least likely to plan for the future or worry about the past. In fact, they have a difficult time remembering the past. You will soon discover that this child has to be punished repeatedly for the same thing.

Good study habits do not come easy for a SanPhleg, neither do good devotional practices. They mean well and often make loud, public commitments to do better, but seldom carry through unless their parents have used the first five years of life to teach them discipline and self-control. If they have a teacher they particularly enjoy, they may do well in that class but poorly in others. A SanPhleg child will do better to study in a room without pictures or anything else to distract him. Otherwise, he will not be able to concentrate.

A high percentage of sanguine children have a weight problem and SanPhlegs probably have it more than any other. They have usually transformed their good physique at birth into a roly-poly body at ten and can anticipate a two-to-five percent increase every year thereafter unless parents help them learn to eat properly. Some children and their parents use the excuse that she or he "has a tendency to gain weight" or "they don't burn their calories off as fast as other children." The truth usually is that they have poor eating habits—eating too fast, eating wrong foods, and eating between meals. Parents can help by teaching their children early in life to enjoy fruits and vegetables, to limit their bread consumption, and to eliminate after-school and bedtime snacks. And by all means, candy, pop, and ice cream should be kept to a minimum. SanPhlegs often have an insatiable sweet tooth. It is easier to curb this problem when they are little than when they are older. Recently we were in a missionary's home where their delightful SanPhleg ten-year-old won my heart. When his mother wasn't looking, I saw him ''stuffing his face'' from the candy dish—and he already carried about fifteen pounds of excess fat.

Weight control, unless there is some organic problem involved, is a self-control and self-discipline problem. Instead of verbalizing discontent about the fact that a child is obese, parents should help him to control his appetite and he will learn self-control in other areas of life as well. We have seen SanPhlegs whose entire lives were transformed into a productive pattern once they conquered their weight problem. The biggest difficulty in helping your child to gain control of his weight is that you have to set a good example or all your training will fail. One brokenhearted mother, sixty-five pounds overweight, recognized her bad eating habits in the life-style of her obese seven-year-old. She was frightened at the prospect of the fulfillment of the old adage, ''like mother, like daughter.''

ChlorSan

The 60 percent choleric and 40 percent sanguine child is not hard to spot. He is an extrovert, though not as extreme as his SanChlor counterpart. But he is a supreme activist and you know he is around! (Don't be confused by the activity patterns of these first four temperament blends during the first years of life—they are all active children.) The thing that distinguishes the ChlorSan is his determination, strong will (in some cases bullheadedness), independence, self-sufficiency, and industry. He usually has only two speeds: Wide open and sound asleep. If very early you start bending that strong will to submit to your authority and teach him to respect others, he will become a more enjoyable child. He has enough charm to sell most anything he sets his mind to—particularly his parents (if he can), on why he should have his own way. Be sure of this, he is out to have his own way and he can be impishly clever in his efforts to obtain it. It is not uncommon for him to start with charm and end up with temper if the charm doesn't work. ChlorSans are good talkers and early in life will argue with their parents. In fact, they can't resist the temptation to get in the last word and this will often be the cause for many of their spankings. Their tendency to justify their actions (whether right or wrong) provides them a ready answer as to why they should break the rules or why the rules should not apply to them.

In school, ChlorSans are generally sports lovers who have to be participants. If they are not fortunate enough to make the team, they usually can be found on the sidelines throwing a football—rarely is he a good spectator in youth. He loves competition and enjoys being at the center of the action. One of his youthful problems is getting home on time. He would rather be punished for being late (if he can't talk you out of it) than leave the ball park early. They are gifted debaters and very argumentative, and that usually shows up by the time he can put three words together.

One of the ChlorSan's traits is being very opinionated and tending to declare himself before weighing the facts and then stubbornly trying to argue his way out of everything. He usually has a fiery temper and both boys and girls will not hesitate to get into a fight. A fourth-grade ChlorSan moved to a new school where the class bully challenged him to a fight. Evenly matched, they both got so tired they had to quit with the promise to resume the next night. That went on for five nights in a row. Finally, the two ChlorSans became the best of friends.

The ChlorSan is not often interested in studies but pursues more active interests. He needs to be guided to use his strong will to control his temper, speak respectfully, stop interrupting others, do his homework and chores, be considerate of the less powerful personalities, and avoid the use of sarcasm. He is the most affectionate of the three choleric blends, but even he rations kisses as if they are scarce. It is extremely important that you lead him to Christ and teach him the importance of being obedient to God early in life. All children should memorize Scripture in their third to sixth grade years when their minds are so impressionable. But the ChlorSan particularly needs to fortify his mind for the rebellious years ahead when he is prone to do his own thing instead of the will of God.

ChlorMel

The ChlorMel child is not only active and productive, but often possesses a razor-sharp mind. Mothers frequently are disappointed that he is not loving, but instead is so independent that he only dispenses affection when he is in the mood. Fathers frequently are unprepared to be rejected by their little ChlorMel daughters and may tend to withdraw from them emotionally. It would be better for the parent to accept the child and his sparse expressions of affection on the child's terms, being careful to always return his love when he is in the mood. These children can learn to love, but it takes time. ChlorMels can be angry, willful, sassy, and sarcastic. They combine the hard to please traits of the choleric and the perfectionism of the melancholic. Their mouth is a dead giveaway when they are rebellious and they need to learn to use it kindly. Proverbs 13:3 says, "He that keepeth his mouth keepeth his life: but he that openeth wide his lips shall have destruction." It takes persistent training to teach them to say "please" and "thank you." One three-year-old ChlorMel girl refused to say please even though her father refused to give her an ice cream cone with the other children until she did. Before she got home she added self-pity to her willfulness and verbalized it so loudly that she well deserved the spanking she received.

No temperament blend can be more independent than the ChlorMel. I saw a two-year-old refuse her grandfather's offer to tie her shoes by saying, "I can do it myself!" In spite of the fact that she didn't know how, she was determined to try. In school the ChlorMels usually do well if taught good study habits and encouraged to balance their insatiable appetite for sports against their need to study. This child will usually come to a place in his life when he refuses to go to church. The wise parent will use that crisis to break this rebellious will as well as to avoid the problem of letting him find his friends outside the church. (Though, frankly, that problem should have been solved long before he got to his teens.)

The secret thought life of a ChlorMel can be very dangerous. He is prone to be an angry child and, together with the revenge and self-persecution tendencies of the melancholic, exaggerates hurts, insults, or problems. Raising a ChlorMel can be a challenging experience, for it is never dull. If the parent of the same sex takes the time to get to know him and be his friend, he will do very well in life provided his strong will and determination are guided toward the control of his tongue, anger, and sarcastic attitude.

ChlorPhleg

The ChlorPhleg is an interesting combination of the hot and cool, providing a moderate temperament for this child. He is the least outgoing of the extroverts and is less likely to go off half-cocked in the wrong direction, for he is more deliberate and organized in everything he does. Once he sets out on a plan, he determinedly follows it through. It is not difficult to guide this child at an early age into taking a paper route or part-time job. He is usually dependable and hardworking and can be an ideal child to raise if he does not develop an attitude of slow-burning inner animosity.

This child provides an interesting combination of the choleric bullheaded determination and the phlegmatic stubbornness. Consequently, it is difficult to get him to change his mind once it is made up. Like the other two cholerics, it is very hard for him to admit when he is wrong, and repentance does not come easy for him. In sports it is hard for him to accept a penalty call by the coach (the coach must be wrong). As a child he must not only be taught to bear the responsibility for his own mistakes, but also to apologize when he has made one. He is a master at getting other children into trouble without implicating himself. Although he is less likely to verbally explode at others and sarcastically cut them to ribbons than the other cholerics, he is more apt to use his phlegmatic humor to disguise it cleverly. He or she can be the nicest little troublemaker on the block. Like all those with a predominantly choleric temperament, he should be led to Christ before his twelfth birthday or he may never show an interest in spiritual things. These children need lots of love and consistent discipline in the home. They are often selfish with their toys and need to be taught early in life to share with others.

MelSan

The first six blends we have examined are predominantly extroverts. Now we shall turn to the more introvert temperaments. You can expect to recognize some similarities between them, except some of their traits will be reversed.

No child is a greater bundle of emotions than the MelSan. He has the capability of going from laughter one moment to sobbing the next. He is naturally insecure and fear prone with an exaggerated guilt complex, so he needs an excessive amount of love and reassurance.

MelSan children are frequently gifted in either I.Q., creativity, art, music, science, or all of these. Strangely enough, they usually have a real problem with self-acceptance in spite of their many talents. If they are subjected to criticism or rejection, it is not uncommon for them to waste their amazing potential. Self-pity is a very dangerous thinking pattern to which he is vulnerable even to the point of being convinced his parents love his brothers and sisters more than they do him.

MelSans are not easy to raise because a parent may often be aware of the child's internal displeasure and criticism even if it is not verbalized. You need to remind yourself that he is usually just as critical of himself as he is of others. One thing you should teach him early is that griping and criticism are not acceptable in your home. He has a keen sensitivity to spiritual things, so if his parents teach him in early childhood to "pray with thanksgiving" and reject his temptations to be critical, it can transform his personality, moodiness, and mental attitude.

Unless gifted in athletics, they will require more than the usual amount of help needed for learning sport skills. You must not allow them to quit just because the sport is difficult for them. When you discover their natural bent toward art or music, it would be wise to get special instruction to help him excel, both for his own self-acceptance and so that God can make better use of his talents.

This child may tend to be anti-social and must be encouraged to make and keep friends. You should particularly seek to get him into group activities—church groups, chorus, band, or sports. Don't be surprised if he comes home and says, "I don't have any friends. Nobody likes me." He is a natural Charlie Brown type that needs to be taught to play with other children, even if he says he doesn't want to. If you have a MelSan, think of him as a diamond given to you by God to polish. Start early; be consistent, understanding and loving; and you will later see him "shine as the stars," for he has a great capacity to serve God.

MelChlor

The MelChlor boy or girl is like plastic clay in the potter's hands. The parent can mold him into a positive and capable person or accentuate his negative feelings until his above-average potential is neutralized. As young children they are often fussier than other temperaments, very demanding and tending to be possessive clingers. It is not uncommon for them to be whiney, selfish, and hard to get along with. Consequently, they may not on the surface be as easy to love as sanguines, but those parents who have made the effort to do so anyway have found it to be a rewarding experience.

The MelChlor child will not be as moody as the MelSan, but his choleric determination will tend to make his bad moods last longer. He seems determined not to give up anything—not even a bad mood. This child usually does not get along well with other children, tends to be selfish, and does not like to share his toys, room, or personal effects. He often feels everyone is against him, and frequently retreats to the solitude of his own room to nurse his grudges. He can be hostile (even when he doesn't express it), and at three years old or sooner he may oppose what you want him to do and the way you want it done.

He may sulk long after punishment, blaming his parent in his mind rather than accepting his own faults. He criticizes himself, but does not like criticism from other people. Even though the choleric element is in a secondary position, its presence in this temperament blend may often give room for negative thinking. When he gets older he will insist that his negativism is "just being realistic." In such a frame of mind he will usually make mountains out of molehills and refuse to take on a chore or project that is well within his capability.

The potential for success of these children can scarcely be overestimated. Watch carefully for the areas of their talents and then give special help to develop them. When they have done something well, give them plenty of approval to keep them going. Gradually their confidence will grow and they will develop rapidly in that field. After that, the thing to watch for is that they do not confine themselves to repeatedly do only the familiar and refuse to venture into other areas and to learn new things. One thing in his favor, he is usually a good student.

The work habits of a MelChlor are never neat, even though he is a natural perfectionist. For that reason you should help him early to keep his room straight and put away his toys. Like the MelSan, he will probably have a critical spirit. If indulged, it will show in his face; conversely, if you teach him the art of thankful living (I Thessalonians 5:18) he will even develop a more cheerful countenance. "A joyful heart makes a cheerful face" (Proverbs 15:13a).

Each new success in his young life will make it easier to experience others unlocking his enormous potential. By looking at him through the rose-colored glasses of what he can become through God's grace, and by lovingly encouraging him to try things he automatically rejects as "too hard," you will help him build a self-image that will enable him to fit more comfortably into society and find a fulfilling service in the Lord's work.

MelPhleg

If you have a MelPhleg child, you may have a budding, young genius on your hands. He won't be as hostile as the previous two melancholic children and will either get along well with other children or will not play with them at all. He is inclined to be a loner, enjoying his own company. As he grows older, he often gets excellent grades and, if accepted lovingly by his parents for what he is, will grow up to be a child of whom you are justifiably proud. But you must avoid trying to make him fit into another kind of mold. Usually he is quiet and subdued, so don't expect a sanguine reaction out of him.

All melancholic children are sensitive, but this one most of all. He may be an emotional "clinger" when he is young. The best thing to do is pray for grace and let him cling. As he gets older he must have a balance of that magic formula for child raising: Love, discipline, acceptance, and Godly instruction. Don't let his "hurt" expressions keep you from punishing him for rebellion, defiance or sass. If applied with love, he will probably get your message earlier than any other temperament.

In spite of his sensitive nature, don't let him get by with selfishness when playing with other children. He is both self-centered and selfish, so he must learn to play with and share with others. Don't be surprised if he is unusually self-conscious; in time he will grow out of most of it. As he grows up, insist that he learn social graces and learn to speak to adults as well as to his own peer group. He would rather "hermit" himself in his room when company comes over, but such a temptation should be discouraged until he has at least greeted guests.

They often have a low threshold for embarrassment. One super sensitive twelve-year-old MelPhleg daughter of a doctor friend of ours ran and hid in the bathroom when her mother first tried to instruct her in the use of a bra. Gradually she came to accept her changing self and today is a lovely wife and mother. Although MelPhlegs need special help developing in the social areas of life, they usually are good students, cause little trouble, and have a responsive heart to spiritual instruction.

PhlegSan

The PhlegSan child is the most unabrasive of all temperaments. When a phlegmatic has a 40 per-cent dose of sanguine charm added, he can be a delightful child. Humanly speaking, these are usually the easiest of all people to get along with. As babies they are happy, contented cuddlers—"the perfect child," so perfect, in fact, that you may be blind to some of their weaknesses. All phlegmatics have a motivational deficiency unless their parents have recognized that trait early and worked on it diligently. Neither the phlegmatic nor the sanguine is overly determined or self-controlled, so self-discipline in every area should be stressed. Don't permit them to leave their toys out overnight. Teach them early the need for keeping their room straight. This child is easy to discipline and usually responds to rewards as well as he does to punishment. What rebellion he possesses should be cured by his third birthday—it just isn't that hard! Lovingly help him over his natural disease of "can't, sir"; that is, don't let him use "I can't" as a cop-out when you know he can, or it will become a lifetime habit causing him to fall short of his capabilities.

The PhlegSan child can be exasperating in school, for although he is capable enough, he never seems to put out to the level of his potential—it seems to take too much effort. He is a natural procrastinator and will often fail to recall his assignment for the next day or his regular "forgetter" has caused him to leave his books at home.

In spite of his congenial ways, he can be stubborn, selfish, and stingy. If he doesn't have brothers and sisters in the home, he will have a hard time learning to share. PhlegSans are timid and shy and need to be drawn out of their shells. But an austere, critical, and loudly demanding parent will drive him deeper into his shell for protection, often inhibiting what social tendencies he might otherwise have. A parent can best help him by teaching him to rely on the Lord and build up his faith through a growing, personal relationship with Jesus Christ.

PhlegChlor

The PhlegChlor is not a great deal different from the PhlegSan except he is even more introversive. He may be fearful and insecure at times. The choleric influence will make him goal-oriented and the most self-motivated of all the phlegmatics, but he will never be a ball of fire. That same influence, however, can also cause him to easily become angry; in fact, of all the phlegmatics he will have the greatest problem with anger. Although he gets along well with others, as do most phlegmatics, he is prone to be stubborn, selfish, and unyielding. This will usually reveal itself in his playing with other children. If he gets into a fight with one, it is usually when the choleric influence in him is activated to protect his toys from being used by others. He tends to preserve them carefully. I know several PhlegChlor men who still have the electric trains of their childhood and they are in good running order.

It will take loving persistence on his parents' part to see that this little PhlegChlor is taught self-control in the form of finishing assignments and fulfilling obligations. The best time to start is between two and three years of age. Beware of T.V.; he can become an addict and live in a television dream world.

When the real world around him becomes unpleasant, he will prefer the false world television provides him.

This child's passive tendencies are compounded by a fear that often stifles his curiosity. He should be encouraged to cultivate his curiosity at a very early age. Although it may try your patience, let him crawl to his heart's content. It helps him later in life to be interested in many things. Parents will need to serve as a motivator for this child, and, frankly, he needs all the motivation he can get. As he becomes an achiever, his fear tendencies will be reduced to life size.

PhlegMel

The most introverted of all twelve temperament blends is the PhlegMel. They are quieter than other children their age. Their crying is usually softer than others unless they are seriously hurt physically or emotionally. Like the other phlegmatic children, they rarely defy you, though they may stubbornly drag their feet. No one can take more time to put their toys or clothes away, and it seems if you would let them, they would sleep all the time. PhlegMels need to be encouraged to assert themselves more, to be given responsible time limits to get jobs done, and to be encouraged to attempt what is within their capabilities. If you don't prod him early in life, he will become a member of the "putterer society" and take forever to get anything done. Between his tendency to get everything organized before he starts something and his perfectionist traits, it usually takes him five times longer to do something than other children. If not cured in childhood, this trait will carry over into adulthood; it will make retaining employment difficult for the PhlegMel man. Housework will be an endless chore for the PhlegMel woman, often keeping her family in a turmoil and enraging an activist husband.

As little tykes, PhlegMels are fearful, insecure, and need lots of love to help them with self-acceptance. The child whose parents reject him will always have a difficult time accepting himself; but that is particularly true of anyone with a degree of melancholic temperament. As a Christian parent, you have divine resources to assist your child with this problem. In fact, much of the Bible is written to help overcome fear, worry, and anxiety. This child (like all others, actually) should be guided to memorize God's Word early and make his faith a vital part of his thinking. Abraham is a good example of a fear-dominated man who became a model of faith.

Conclusion

This brief application of the twelve blends in temperaments is not meant to be exhaustive. It is intended to help you see that every child has talents, strengths and weaknesses, and should be considered in the light of his own individuality. Hopefully this concept will help you diagnose both your child's primary and secondary temperaments and help you set goals that you wish to accomplish in the light of his needs. You should develop a plan in advance designed to lovingly help him strengthen his weaknesses. Many parents make the mistake of treating all their children alike, and in so doing, often stifle latent creativity that should have been developed. Others have no plan for child rearing, but expect to make up their mind on the spot as problems arise. We don't do that in baking, sewing, or anything else. Why should we be haphazard about the important task of child growing? As they say in business, "Make your plan and work your plan"—you will enjoy your final product much more.

One Christian psychologist who is employed by a number of industrial corporations as a free lance consultant told us that his approach was to concentrate on a person's strengths and ignore their weaknesses. He studied people carefully for industry to make sure that they were temperamentally suited for the task they were assigned; then he encouraged them to concentrate on developing their strengths in the fulfillment of that task. His assumption was that their weaknesses would automatically take care of themselves. We do not fully concur with this theory, but instead believe that in Galatians 5:22, 23, the Holy Spirit provides every human being a strength for every conceivable weakness. These available spiritual resources should be used in the development of Christian children. However, that Christian psychologist's success in industry certainly underscores that every good parent should find the area of his children's natural talents and strengths so that he can help them cultivate and develop a high degree of proficiency. Your child will like himself better when you give him that help. If he likes himself more, you will find it easier for you to like him and for others to enjoy him. But the greatest result of encouraging him to develop his strengths and to overcome his weaknesses is that he will be more usable in the hand of God for whatever the perfect will of his Heavenly Father might be for his life.

5

Through The Diaper And Crayola Days

Mother's Great Adjustments

The first baby presents a terrific adjustment for the mother. The reality of her new role in life does not hit her until she comes home from the hospital and there she is—face to face with this brand new, breathing baby. It has come to stay twenty-four hours a day, and it won't go away! Most new mothers are scared when they realize that they now have the full responsibility for the life of this tiny human being.

A new mother may feel so inadequate and unsure of herself that she tends to worry about every little thing. If the baby is sleeping, she checks often to see if he is breathing. If he cries, she is concerned that he is ill. Such insecurity may cause her some tension at times, but she would die before she would admit these feelings to anybody else. If only she knew that most new mothers tend to feel the same way! She thinks that every other mother has a natural "mother instinct" and that she must be the only one that does not.

In addition to the new mother's feelings of inadequacy, there's another set of feelings which bother her a great deal—feelings of resentment. This resentment can be the result of being tied down and not free to go and come as she did formerly. Her time is no longer her own. She suddenly has a little creature that demands a lot of care and attention. The new twenty-four-hour-a-day schedule causes many new mothers to become resentful. This is entirely normal, but unfortunately nobody has prepared her for this portion of her new experience.

Another factor which may cause a mother to resent her new baby is that she assumes that a child will automatically bring her and her husband closer together, and quite the opposite happens. Instead of bringing them together, the innocent new baby may act as a wedge which separates them. The husband is often jealous of the attention given to the new baby. His wife's time used to belong to him. He may also have the opinion that 100 percent of the responsibility is hers and he is shoved out in the cold.

The Christian young couple must accept these emotions as part of the normal adjustment period for both the husband and wife. Each mother will need to find her own ideas and methods of making this threesome a close unit. It will help her to remember that these feelings of inadequacy, resentment, and panic are all very normal, and as she gains experience, her confidence will grow.

"An Original Created by God"

As we develop this chapter, let me remind you of the uniqueness of your baby. There is no one else in the world like your child. He is literally one of a kind. His particular combination of genes has never before existed and will never exist again. His label can read, "An original created by God." So if your baby's development does not match the time schedule of the "typical" baby found in many books, don't jump to the conclusion that there is something wrong with him. Please don't try to force him into some mental picture you have read in a book of what the "average" baby ought to be like. Let him be unique!

Your role as a parent is of extreme importance to help your child develop this uniqueness. He needs your help and encouragement. If you can accept his individual patterns of eating and sleeping, his babyish temperament and moods, it will be easier for you to accept his individuality at later stages of development.

You will be a happier parent if you give up trying to make your child fit into your own image. Give him the freedom to develop naturally according to his temperament.

Different Stages of Development

Each child goes through the same general stages of development and in the same order but on a different time schedule. The most important stages in development will be during the first few years of his life. You are programming him for a high level of intellectual attainment. This period in his life moves in a furious pace never to be equalled again in a similar period. One-half of the intellectual capacity of an adult has been developed by the age of four and 80 percent by the age of eight (this is intelligence, not information). After that, with schooling and environment, his mental abilities can be altered only 20 percent.

The following four stages during the development of your child list only an approximate time schedule. Remember, your child is unique—one of a kind.

I. Infancy (Birth to One Year)

His learning begins at the moment of his birth. The infant is never too young to learn anything. He acquires his basic outlook on life and is developing either a basic sense of trust and happiness or one of distrust and unhappiness. The environment you provide for him will play a large role in determining what his self-concept will be.

A. FIRST THREE MONTHS. There are seven basic needs that an infant has during this period of development. The fulfillment of these needs will be the beginning of teaching him basic trust and a good self-concept.

1. *Hunger*—Infants seem to be all mouth and stomach, but a baby feels intense hunger pangs. After he has been fed, he will go back to sleep until the hunger pangs wake him up again. As he grows older he will have longer periods of wakefulness. His

hunger can be easily satisfied by simply feeding him. The great controversy is whether it should be breast feeding or bottle feeding. Isn't it a shame that we have complicated something that was designed to be so simple? God designed a mother's breast to produce milk only after giving birth to a baby. There is no option given in the Bible because there are no alternatives. The benefit of breast-feeding is that it automatically involves cuddling and stroking, which are necessary ingredients in the development of each child. Unfortunately, the bottle-fed baby often has his bottle propped up when mother gets too busy to sit down and hold him. You have the freedom to choose the method you will use; but if you choose bottle-feeding, be certain you can discipline yourself to hold and cuddle your baby for every feeding, or you will be depriving him of an important ingredient for proper development.

Now the question comes up: When to feed your baby? Should he be fed on a rigid time schedule or simply when he gets hungry? Remember that he is an original creation and a time schedule that suits one baby may not be satisfying to another. Each baby's hunger may vary from day to day. When he is hungry he becomes frustrated. He wants to be fed "now." One medical doctor says that when a baby has to wait a half hour for his feeding, it is as if an adult had to wait three days. When the infant is hungry and is not fed, he reacts by crying. The longer he waits, the louder and more insistent his crying becomes. As more time passes, the crying changes in quality and tone. Now his crying takes on a tone of anger. He is furious because no one is paying any attention to him. Finally, he begins to learn that no amount of crying will bring attention to his needs. He may react with continued anger or he may become listless and apathetic, weakened and resigned that no one will respond. Whichever he chooses, he has learned a basic distrust of life.

How much better it would be for the child if you would respect his individuality from birth. You can help build the foundation for a strong and healthy self-concept if you would feed him when he is hungry.

2. *Warmth*—This is one area that most parents do not need

to be reminded about. In fact, many pediatricians claim that some young mothers overdress infants so they are kept too warm. The important thing to remember is that babies should not be allowed to get chilled. Wind is one chill factor to which small babies should not be exposed.

3. *Sleep*—The baby will take care of this need himself if the first two needs have been cared for. When he has had enough sleep, he will wake up. It is a good habit not to keep the house hushed for the baby to sleep. Keep the noise in the house at a reasonable, normal volume and the baby will develop the ability to sleep in these surroundings.

Occasionally a baby may wake up crying during the middle of the night for some unknown reason. He may have stomach distress or colic, which you can do nothing about. Your stroking or cuddling may not comfort him or stop the crying. Moments like these will be very trying on the young parents. In the wee hours of the morning you may feel frustrated, panicky, or even angry that your sleep has been disturbed and that you can do nothing for the child. If your feelings get out of control and you find yourself hitting or yelling at the baby, then I advise you to leave the room immediately and get alone to confess this anger to God. If you cannot control your feelings at a time like this, then you should seek the aid of a minister who can help and advise you before you bring bodily harm to a helpless child.

4. *Physical Cuddling and Stroking*—Unless your baby experiences being rocked, cuddled, stroked, talked to and sung to, he cannot know he is loved. It must be demonstrated in a physical way. As you rock your infant, the soft tone of mother's voice as she gently sings to him will help him to know he is loved. Love him all you want! Loving never "spoiled" any baby.

5. *Bodily Exercise*—There is a limit to what this little fellow can do in the way of bodily exercise. However, there should be a certain period during the day when he is allowed to swing his arms and legs freely without being swaddled with blankets. While traveling through South America I observed many different tribes of Indians who dressed their infants in swaddling clothes with arms and legs wrapped snugly in a

down-stretched position. There was no room for movement of any kind. Even up to the age of two or more they are most often strapped on the mother's back with little or no leg exercise at all. Just as you must gradually develop their minds intellectually, so their physical bodies need this day-by-day development of their limbs with exercise.

6. *Diaper Attention*—Attend to the changing of diapers with a matter-of-fact attitude. The parent who communicates dislike and disapproval toward the messy diaper may succeed in making the job of toilet training more difficult later on. You will profit by taking a more relaxed attitude toward diaper changing. As long as the infant is not in a cold room, he will probably not be bothered by a wet or messy diaper. This does not mean that you should neglect him so that he develops a bad case of diaper rash, but it does mean that there is no need to awaken him just to change a diaper that may seem unpleasant to you.

7. *Sensory and Intellectual Stimulation*—Each child inherits a certain maximum intelligence potential which he might reach as he grows up. However, whether or not he reaches his maximum intelligence will depend a great deal on how much sensory and intellectual stimulation he receives in the first few years of his life. He needs to be able to handle objects that he can smell, hear, put in his mouth, and even suck. Care must be given to see that he does not have access to objects which are small enough for him to choke on.

B. THREE TO SIX MONTHS. This period is a time of transition from infancy to babyhood. He will begin to investigate his world by reaching out to things. He explores his environment with his eyes, ears and mouth. At this age everything starts to go into his mouth to be tested. This is his method of discovering things around him. His hands are used to grasp and feel objects and then to explore them further by trying them in his mouth. Don't be alarmed if he begins to suck his fingers. This is a built-in pacifier that God has given him to keep him quiet so he can learn about the sights and sounds of his new world. The fetus has already achieved hand-to-mouth contact before birth, so look on it as a normal step in this stage of development.

Rattles and rubber squeeze toys are good at this stage. Examine them carefully to be certain there are no detachable parts that your baby could swallow. A contrasting texture for him would be soft, cuddly toys.

This is about the only period when a child can be confined to a playpen. He is too young to move himself about, but he enjoys being around other people. After this stage he wants the freedom of maneuvering himself from place to place.

C. SIX TO NINE MONTHS. Give your baby time to adjust to a new situation. Proceed slowly when you are showing him a new person. If the introduction results in crying, he is telling you that he is afraid. It is quite common at this stage to develop an anxiety toward strangers. During this period his babbling and vocalizing will increase. He will probably expose his first tooth and he may even become an active member of the family by crawling. He has learned a form of communication of his very own. Through grunts and gestures he can usually indicate what he wants. Water play is probably the most soothing and relaxing activity for a baby at this age. He enjoys splashing but is still unsteady; so the water must be kept shallow to prevent him from having a fearful experience or even drowning. Do not leave him unattended. At this age baby should not be kept in the playpen but should be allowed a corner of a room where there is nothing that could endanger him. He can often play happily by himself for a half-hour at a time. He enjoys playing with simple household objects such as plastic dishes or cups.

D. NINE TO TWELVE MONTHS. At this stage your baby may already be walking, or he may not start for a few more months. He will no longer be passive and quiet while you are changing a diaper or dressing him. He will begin to show unsophisticated coordination with games such as patty-cake. Your baby will be able to understand a great many things that are said to him. You can teach him by speaking to him in single words when you are identifying objects.

This is the time to introduce books to your child. He will probably put them in his mouth, but remember that is the way he explores new objects. His books should be made of cloth or heavy cardboard and should be filled with simple pictures and single words. Let him taste or pat or stroke the pages. Your proper response to this will lay the foundation for his love and appreciation for good books.

II. Toddlers (One to Two Years)

The toddler stage begins as soon as your baby learns to walk. This is a great day for him because now he can explore areas of the house that he could not reach before. Even when he was crawling, he was rather limited where he could go or how fast he could get there, but now new worlds are open to him for exploration.

A. CHILD-PROOF THE HOUSE. While he is learning to explore new things, you will be busy learning how to child-proof the house for your baby's protection. At this point a mother has to decide which she wants—a spotless house and a toddler who is passive and full of self-doubts, or a somewhat littered house and a toddler who has a good self-esteem and developing self-confidence. Too often toddlers are raised in a house designed for adults, and their curiosity and desire to explore is held back with restraint. The curiosity that the toddler shows at this stage is the same curiosity which will make him successful in school and his occupation in later life. He needs to be guarded so as not to bring harm to himself, but do not restrain his desire for wanting to learn. Remove the dangerous and breakable objects from his reach. The experts tell us that safety precautions to child-proof your house could prevent 50 to 90 percent of the accidents which seriously injure or kill babies and toddlers.

B. PROTECTED BUT NOT OVERPROTECTED. This faster moving baby needs to be protected but not overprotected. There is a vast difference. He needs parents to protect him against dangers he is too naive to guard against. But if a situation holds no danger, you are being overprotective and this will fill your child with fear and will definitely affect his ability to cope with the world. Abnormal fears can be instilled in your child's emotions by the way you protect him and react to situations in life.

C. FINGER SUCKING. If your child has been a finger-sucker during his first year, you can expect that it will taper off slightly in his second year. He will be more active and will be able to entertain himself with a greater variety of things. When he or she becomes tired, unhappy, or bored, you can expect that the fingers will go back into the mouth again. I encourage mothers to introduce a blanket or stuffed animal to their child and hope that it will become a replacement for finger sucking. There is no shame in seeing a young child able to invest some of his ability to love and care for a doll, teddy bear, or even a worn out, soft blanket. He should be able to count on this source of comfort when he needs it—and for as long as he needs it. Don't be concerned that your little "Linus" will grow up to take his blanket to college. If your attitude toward his blanket has been normal and not disapproving, then he will make the adjustment in due time. As children mature they seem to be able to satisfy these needs with relationships to other people and to involve themselves in things that are more interesting.

D. EATING HABITS. Even at this young age many parents are allowing their children to develop atrocious eating habits. I have walked through a grocery store on many occasions and watched while mothers with small children in their carts have loaded their baskets with sugars, starches, and prepared foods that have little or no food value. Excesses of the sugars and starches will contribute to decay of the teeth and sometimes even to diabetes. Not only are these foods harmful in themselves but they also satisfy the appetite and keep children from eating foods that are more valuable. Parents of babies and young children have the opportunity to start their children off with good eating habits right from the start. Make the diet so good and the rule so definite that the children accept them as a matter of course, particularly in these early years when their bodies are developing and need the benefits of good dietary habits. There can be exceptions for occasional treats, but they should be held to a minimum.

Youngsters often become choosy and finicky about their food at this age and may eat less. This is probably a blessing because if they continued eating at the same rate as the first year of life, they would be as wide as they were tall. Also, his appetite will vary from day to day just as his parents' will. Mother, don't fret or feel worried that your child is not eating enough! All too often mothers will worry about little Betsy not eating her vegetables. The more she pressures little Betsy to eat vegetables, the more Betsy balks. The less the child eats, the more worried and anxious mother becomes, until finally the mother has a full-fledged eating problem on her hands where before no problem existed. This is completely unnecessary. Remember, a mother has on her side the natural hunger of the child. Offer Betsy a well-balanced diet and leave her alone. Sooner or later her hunger pangs will take over and she will eat what you offer her. Be sure you are not offering snacks of sweets and starches. Give her the freedom to turn against certain foods. Without making an issue of the matter she may decide next week that it is her very favorite.

Sometimes during this stage of development your child will decide that he wants to spoon-feed himself. There is only one way for him to learn and that is to take the spoon and begin. It takes a lot of drips and spills to accomplish this, but it is a great step toward independence.

E. TOILET TRAINING. Most American mothers are in a great hurry to get rid of the diaper routine, and why not? It is a nuisance to always take spare diapers everywhere you go, not to mention the mess and the odor. It is a great day when a child has graduated from diaper wearing and can take care of his own detail. But to try to toilet train too early can be a psychological disaster, or at least a waste of the mother's time and efforts. One noted medical doctor has said that a child does not have the neuro-muscular maturation he needs to control his bladder and bowels until after two years of age. He even went so far as to say that whenever he finds a youngster over the age of five who is a bed wetter, it is quite probable that the toilet training of the child was mishandled in some way. Another well-respected child psychologist states that a child is not ready for bowel control before his second year or for urinary control before his third year. He adds that a child is not considered a bed wetter until the age of five years. So be patient, dear mother, and remind yourself with every diaper you change that you are helping your child to develop a normal adulthood.

F. EDUCATING WITH TOYS. Books are a very important part of his life at this stage. He will still need books that are made of cloth or heavy cardboard because he will undoubtedly investigate them by tearing or chewing on them. You can begin reading simple nursery rhymes or Bible story books geared to the toddler's age level. He will soon be able to identify single words from a story that is repeated over and over such as "Jesus" when he sees a baby in a manger.

There are numerous playthings available that help to develop his large and small muscles. A few examples are a low slide, small jungle gym, sandbox with pail and shovel, pail of water for making mud pies, cuddly animals, dolls, and music that deals with sounds and rhythm.

G. SPANKING. Spanking a two-year-old is very necessary at times, but be careful not to falsely interpret the behavior of the toddler as being hostile or destructive. It may be that he is just exercising his curiosity and acting in normal behavior for his age. A two-year-old child may be unable to understand adult reasoning when he reaches out to play with an electric wall plug. He is too young to suffer natural consequences, so a spanking is obviously necessary in this case. His derriere will be well padded with diapers, so a sting on the hands as he reaches out to touch the wall plug will remind him that that was an unpleasant experience without giving him bodily harm.

The first signs of temperament traits may begin to reveal themselves during this stage. The wise parent will be alert and will deal with them to best help the child.

The choleric toddler will show signs of being a bully to other children, very selfish with his toys, and definitely beginning to show a strong self-will. This young child needs to have his will broken but not his spirit. Too many parents excuse this behavior by saying that Cindy would be different if she had a brother or sister, but in reality that would probably make no difference—she is just acting like a choleric. Her great need is to have parents who are willing to deal with that selfishness and to discipline her with strong, consistent training. After three years of age that will becomes harder to break with each passing year.

The sanguine toddler will have a hot temper and may reveal it by screaming and turning bright red in the face as his body stiffens. His anger can flare up so fast that before the watchful eye of the parent he can pick up a toy and fling it at the one who angered him. In spite of his copious tears of remorse, this uncontrollable anger needs to be dealt with as soon as it is displayed and before he becomes dangerous. He cannot be permitted to harm other children with his fits of rage.

The phlegmatic toddler will remain rather passive at this age and will be more of an observer than a participant. His weaknesses will take a bit longer before they begin to show and will probably make him an easier child to deal with at this stage.

The melancholic toddler can be recognized by his whining disposition and is the one who is inclined to be more of a clinger when left at Grandma's or with a baby-sitter. This child needs to be loved and given a sense of security more than the others. Make sure that spankings given are only for direct acts of rebellion and followed with love and tenderness that assure the child of your forgiveness. The parent needs to be very sensitive to what best helps the child and what is really behind the whining and clinging—gaining his way or real insecurity.

H. CONCLUSION. The experts tell us that between birth and five years of age children alternate years in being difficult to raise and cope with. In other words, the odd years (one-three-five) seem to be the years when a child is generally a pleasure to have around while the even years (two-four) are the trying years when the child is in a transition stage and acts more like an obnoxious monster than an adorable child. Probably most parents would agree that the age of two and one-half years is the most exasperating time of a child's preschool training. Remember, just about the time you feel that you can't live with this little unreasonable monster, he will turn three and begin to change for the better.

III. Trusty Threes

Now you can begin to expect a new spirit of cooperation from the more pleasant three-year-old. Prior to this, one might think that the child, instead of the parents, was running the family. But if you have responded properly to his demands of control, you should now begin to have a more enjoyable home environment. The three-year-old seems to have a desire to win the approval of his older sisters and brothers and also his parents. He is more able to work patiently at dressing himself or at similar tasks instead of exploding as he may have done previously. He has a greater ability to interact with other children in sharing and taking turns.

This should be a delightful time for both parents and child because he is more content. He loves his parents, he enjoys life, and he is generally at peace with the world. However, I would not want to deceive you into thinking your troubles are over. They may be lessened, but there are still challenges ahead as your child moves toward maturity.

At the age of three he begins to crave playmates for companionship. His desire for independence will cause him to want limited separations from his mother. Moms should not feel threatened when this occurs because this is a normal part of their development. He still wants the security and protection of the mother but needs some independence and companionship with his peers.

This is an important step for your child and needs to be handled very matter-of-factly. He needs to learn how to cope with short periods of separation in order to build toward longer periods when school begins. He should be encouraged to venture out to play with the neighborhood children, or if there is a good nursery school near you, then I would suggest letting him attend for three to four hours a week at the beginning. Notice that I am suggesting limited short periods of separation. I do not recommend children be enrolled in a full-time nursery school at this young age. Too much of their development is based on the mother-child relationship, even at three years.

As the child enters the third year there will be a swinging back and forth from the extreme independence of "I can do it myself" attitude to the limp and helpless "I can't do it" and mother must do it for him. It is wise for parents to have consistent rules and limits at this stage, but do not make too many demands for absolute conformity. However, he must learn to conform to what his parents and society expect of him and at the same time develop a healthy self-identity. You must weigh the limits and demands carefully. They should be reasonable and consistent and you should be able to justify these limits to yourself and to your child.

At this young age we need not be rigid about what is "feminine" or "masculine." There is no harm in allowing a three-year-old girl to play with trucks and fire engines, if that is what she wants; and there is no harm in a three-year-old boy playing house or dolls if he chooses. Many mothers provide old dress-up clothes for the girls to engage in imaginary dramatic play, but what about the boys? Usually if they desire to play they must wear the dresses, hats, and high-heeled shoes. If you provide some of father's old jeans, hats, and boots, then he can enter the dramatic performance as a man. However, don't be alarmed if he should choose to wear the dress one day for the next day he will probably prefer the jeans. Such choices do not indicate that he will be abnormal. The important factor is Mother and Father's attitude toward the little girl or boy. If Mom and Dad make over the daughter's femininity with her docile, sweet spirit and ruffle her curls, then the son deserves equal attention regarding his nature of boyish toughness and mischievousness.

The most important person in a young child's life is his mother, so both boys and girls tend to identify with her from the very beginning. After all, up to this time, they have spent the major portion of each day of their life with her. Little boys and little girls, too, since they love their mother, want to be like her. However, most boys and girls begin to branch off into their own separate psychological development. It is very important for fathers to spend time with their preschool sons to compensate for this lack of male influence (preschool daughters need the male relationship also). This early contact with your children will build good father-and-son or father-and-daughter relationships for later years. Both little girls and little boys need models to imitate.

A. TOO MUCH OR TOO LITTLE CONTROL. The melancholic and choleric parent will tend to be more rigid and domineering than the other temperaments. Their demands can be far too numerous, and it results in overcontrolling their children. The mother with the newly waxed kitchen floor or the freshly hung bathroom towels needs to remember that the house should be designed for the children, not the children for the house. Parental overcontrol is not very tolerant of childish impulses and emotional outbursts typical of children this age. The responses will vary, depending greatly on the temperament of each child.

1. *The Sanguine Child*—This type of overcontrol will be bitterly resisted by the sanguine, and through his tears he will spout off loudly because of the unreasonable restrictions put on him. This whole stage of development becomes a battleground of wills between parent and child, and regardless of who wins the battle, the child loses the potential of developing his individuality at this stage. This may well be the beginning of producing a rebellious child.

2. *Choleric Child*—The choleric child may be able to control his outward feelings more than the sanguine, but inwardly he will resist it just as bitterly and will hold out to the bitter end rather than give in. Unfortunately, he will become frustrated and eventually rebellious because he is not able to develop his own temperament and be himself.

3. *Phlegmatic Child*—This temperament may respond without any unpleasant confrontations. However, the final result could well be the development of a quiet, passive, fearful child who easily could become a timid, unaggressive adult afraid to venture out and try new things. Since this temperament tends to be fearful anyway, he needs encouragement to be more assertive rather than to be held down.

4. *Melancholic Child*—This child may appear to conform to the parental overcontrol, but inwardly he will seethe with hostility. He will grudgingly do what is expected of him, but will become sneaky and do his own thing. His hostility may be shown in destroying something valuable or pinching baby brother. The melancholic may grow up to be a narrow-minded,

self-righteous person, outwardly full of pious, moral rules, but inwardly full of hostility.

Equally harmful to a three-year-old is the problem of too little control from the parents. The sanguine and phlegmatic parents will be most guilty of this—the phlegmatic because they are loving and do not like confrontations, and the sanguine because they are happy-go-lucky, inconsistent, and have an everything-is-going-to-work-out-okay attitude. When their children refuse to abide by the limits and controls set, they immediately relax the limits and let their children have their own way. Soon the children play the role of parent and take over the control of the house. These children are going to have a difficult time when they enter school and find that the teacher and the children require a reasonable amount of conformity to the rules. Parents can greatly aid their children's adjustment to school and society by helping them learn to conform to rules at home.

B. TOILET TRAINING. This section is not designed to give you specific instructions on how to toilet train your child. There are numerous books available written by medical doctors who go into great detail on this subject. I would like to consider the affects of improper toilet training and your attitudes toward teaching this new skill.

It is needless to say that you cannot toilet train your child unless he is willing to be trained. The old adage "you can lead a horse to water but you can't make him drink" can be related to toilet training also. "You can lead a child to the toilet but you can't make him go." The motivating power that causes him to give up his old, convenient method of elimination is his good relationship with his mother. He enjoys being rewarded by her love and attention when he succeeds in this new way of life. Successful toilet training requires a good relationship between mother and child.

If you put pressure on him to learn too fast and you have not slowly paved the way, then he could easily feel helpless and frustrated. This is a complex undertaking for a child. Punishment for failures or accidents can produce fear, anger, stubbornness, and even defiance in the child. Punishment should never be used in toilet training.

A few simple suggestions for mothers regarding toilet training are to approach it in a casual and relaxed manner. Be matter-of-fact and do not be in a hurry. Even though every kid in the block was toilet trained when he was the age of your child, you must remember that your son or daughter is unique. He is an individual. He will make a lot of mistakes, but we all do when we are learning a new skill.

C. BEDTIME RITUAL. Children at this age love rituals, so to make bedtime a more enjoyable experience, it is a good idea to establish a "bedtime ritual." This can be a very beneficial time when the father can share in preparing the child for bed each night. Unfortunately, this is not a very good time for rough play since it overstimulates the child and makes it hard for him to go to sleep and may even produce restlessness during the night. The ideal time would be to have active play as soon as the father gets home from work in the afternoon and before dinner. This could be anything from rolling or catching a ball to wrestling on the floor. If you cannot work out this ideal schedule, and since rough play is of great value between father and child, you may have to work it in after dinner. A brief period could be designated for active play (maybe ten minutes).

Then proceed to the tub for a bath. Most children look at the bath time simply as playing and Dad could take advantage of that and supervise the bath with boats and floating toys. After the pajamas are on is an ideal time for book reading or story telling. Dad may desire to enter the picture at this point and perform the nightly ritual of telling or reading a story, or even making up a story if he is so inclined. Children love made-up stories with funny noises. The last story should be a comforting Bible story such as Jesus loving the little children, the little lost lamb, or Jesus as a baby in the manger. Then let him pray. Children love to talk to Jesus in their own simple, floundering way. They have great faith and expectations, so build on it. A goodnight kiss and a hug will finish it off for the night. All this ritual can take from 40 to 60 minutes depending on what all you include. One father complained when I told him that the "bedtime ritual" could take about 60 minutes and I suggested he do it with his child. He felt he didn't have that time to give, yet the same dad could find time later in the evening to sit for 60 minutes and watch "Kojak" or "Charlie's Angels" on T.V. There are only a few years when you can tuck them into bed and give them that goodnight kiss. And many a parent wishes they had been more faithful while they had the opportunity.

Bedtime should be a time of pleasure for the child and you want him to look forward to this fun experience. You do not want him to dread or fear it, but some children may because they are afraid of the dark. Don't send him to a dark room if he is afraid. If a soft light in his room will eliminate this fear, then by all means let him have light. You need not worry that he will grow up always needing a light in his room. As he grows older he will overcome many of these childish fears if you've been understanding and considerate of him at this age.

D. QUESTIONS, THEN ANSWERS. One of the greatest gifts you can give your little child is to share with him your knowledge of the world as you answer his questions. The most ideal response would be that a parent answer all the questions a child shall ask; however, no parent is able to answer every question asked at this age. Don't feel guilty if occasionally you suggest that he play quietly so that you can have time to think. But if a mother realized the value of these questions and her answers, she might be able to have a better attitude toward them. This interchange between mother and child may be teaching some of the most important courses on everyday living that he will ever experience.

Many parents live very busy lives. When they are too busy to listen to their children, then they are *too* busy. The parents who want to be successful in child raising will have to discipline themselves to listen. When they do, they are assuring the child that they really care about him and that they think he is important. This is the way to build a good self-image in your child. You will also learn what is going on in his mind if you listen carefully to what he has to say. Being alert to his talk may give you sufficient warning when fears or insecurities begin to build up in his thoughts.

The parents of a sanguine child will have to do more listening because the sanguine does more talking. The phlegmatic child is not too talkative, so his parents will have to be sensitive regarding what he does not talk about. It is wise parents who will encourage him to talk and to express himself, and they can best accomplish this by listening to him.

E. FIRST IMAGE OF HEAVENLY FATHER. A little child relates unknown things to what he knows. He first hears about the Heavenly Father but cannot see Him, so he relates this unknown father to his earthly father whom he knows. This is not restricted to just the age of three. It is mentioned here because this is where it begins, but it will carry on for the next few years. He learns of God's love by watching you. He learns of God's mercy and forgiveness by watching you. Be sure you are giving him an honest picture of what he can expect from his own Heavenly Father.

F. BOOKS. Books for this age should be well constructed. Just because they go in the mouth, do not be deceived into thinking he is too young to profit from books. One of the earliest ways to stimulate him intellectually is by reading to him and acquainting him with the great wealth of knowledge that comes from books.

A child in this stage is fascinated by words and word play. He will love nursery rhymes with their rhythm and repetition of sounds. He likes familiar nursery tales such as *Chicken Little* or the *Three Little Pigs*. He will be able to recognize what is coming next in the story and say it with you as you read to him.

He enjoys looking at the book and touching it. Ask him questions about the story or ask him to find things in the illustrations. He will love it. Most often he will have a favorite book that he will want you to read to him every day. If you change one phrase he will object and correct you.

A few other good books are:

The Cat in the Hat Beginner Book Dictionary, Doctor Seuss, (Random House).
The Giant Nursery Book of Things That Go, George Zaffo, (Doubleday).
Goodnight, Moon, Margaret Wise Brown, (Harper & Row).

Tall Book of Nursery Tales illustrated by Feodor Rojankovsky, (Harper & Row).
The Tale of Peter Rabbit, Beatrix Potter, (Warne).
Millions of Cats, Wanda Gag, (Coward-McCann).
Series of *Pattibooks*, Mary E. LeBar, (Scripture Press).

This list is very scanty, but it is only intended to create an appetite to research the vast number of books available for your toddler. It is inaccurate to place books in age categories because maturity and understanding vary so much. Parents, examine every book carefully before bringing it home to read to your child. You alone can determine what will best suit him.

The experience can be a pleasure to both reader and listener when you have a little, warm body sitting snugly beside you and together you go off to the adventure that a good book provides. It is an experience to remember.

IV. Frisky Fours

Suddenly the three-year-old who has made great strides and has been well coordinated may now begin to demonstrate almost a reversal in his coordination. It may show in such things as picking his nose, biting his nails, or sucking his thumb.

He loves to play with other children his age, even though he may not get along with them too well. His relationships may be stormy and violent, filled with demands, shoving, and hitting. There is often a good deal of bossiness and belligerence in the four-year-old, and his emotional extremes may vary from shyness one moment to boisterousness the next.

He has also learned that there are a whole group of words that his parents do not approve of, and he can usually get attention when using them.

This seems to be a period of testing authority because he loves to defy orders or requests. Because of this, four-year-olds need firmness. Their scrapping can best be dealt with by social isolation. The parent should matter-of-factly say, "You and Chris do not play very well this morning so you will need to play by yourself now. You will be able to play together when I think you can play peaceably again." This will be a motivating factor for him to shape up so he can return to his friends.

I agree with a noted child psychologist when he stated that a four-year-old reminded him of the man described by Stephen Leacock, who jumped on his horse and rode off rapidly in all directions. The four-year-old does not know where he is going even though he is filled with activity. He can be a confused blend of silly and serious, quiet and noisy, cheerful and whiney, indifferent and cooperative, agreeable and disagreeable, shy and aggressive.

A. DEVELOPING PHYSICALLY AND INTELLECTUALLY. Because of the great need for the biological development of Mr. Frisky Four, he has an intense drive to release his energy. He needs to climb, wiggle, run, jump, and yell to accomplish this. Therefore, he needs to have constructive outlets for his energy, otherwise he will find destructive ones. Parents have difficulty accepting this because their needs are for peace and quiet. If you give your child ample opportunity to run, jump, climb, or crawl, you will be aiding his intellectual skills when he starts to school. (For a more thorough study on this you might consult the book by Radler & Kephart entitled *Success Through Play*.)

B. TEMPER TANTRUMS. All children are capable of having a temper tantrum regardless of their temperament. However, the sanguine will be the most likely to scream at the top of his lungs and throw himself on the floor in a fit of rage. The choleric has this potential if he has had little discipline. But the melancholic can muster up a good tantrum if he feels like he has been dealt with unjustly. The most unlikely tantrum-thrower would be the phlegmatic since he is rather passive and peace loving. But any child who becomes so enraged that all he can do is cry, scream, or throw himself on the floor will have a temper tantrum.

If you give in to his demands during a tantrum, you will reinforce it and teach him to throw another tantrum the next time he wants his way. This outburst of emotion results from the struggle for power within him. When he emerges victorious in such a struggle, the child has learned that he can gain control by throwing tantrums. Contrary to what many others have said, I firmly believe the most effective method of handling a tantrum is to respond to his anger. A parent should, first of all, be sure he himself is filled with the Holy Spirit (meaning not to act in rage or frustration), then firmly send the child to his room until he has calmed down and gained control of himself. When the temper fit has ended, then the parent can better communicate with the child and point out his uncalled-for behavior and respond with a sound spanking. A spanking given in the midst of the tantrum results in a further struggle for power. Do not allow yourself to be brought into that struggle. The great temptation is to raise your voice and scream at your child for his behavior. When you respond in that way, you have lost—you have lost the struggle and you have lost control of the situation.

C. BEGINNING SEX EDUCATION. The age at which children begin to ask questions will vary a great deal. Some observant children will notice very early that girls sit and boys stand when they go to the bathroom, or that boys have an extra part that girls don't have. However, there will be some who will be oblivious to the difference at this age. One little boy was looking at a very small nude infant waiting for his bath. His mother, also watching, asked her son if the baby was a girl or a boy. He quickly responded, "I can't tell when his clothes are off."

The important thing to remember about this subject is to face questions with a calm, matter-of-fact attitude. This will be the greatest contribution you can make to your child's sexual development. Answer each question as it comes and answer it honestly. When your four-year-old daughter discovers that her brother has a penis, matter-of-factly call it a penis, just as you would identify his knee or toe.

Some little girls may feel that they have been short-changed by not having a penis. Occasionally, a little boy may become fearful that his may get cut off like his sister's was. A mother's healthy attitude toward these fears in children can help to make them short-lived. I appreciated what one medical doctor suggested as an answer to both boys and girls to help them accept with confidence their bodies as they are. Simply explain to your boy or girl that fathers and boys have a penis and mothers and girls have a special bag built inside their tummy called a uterus. This bag is a special place where God makes babies grow. This should satisfy their questions for the time; but, believe me, more questions will come.

D. AFFECTS OF TV WATCHING. Statistics prepared by the A. C. Neilson Company, the television rating and research firm, show that boys and girls between the ages of two and five watch an average of 23¼ hours of television a week with the figure going down in the summer and up in the winter. Furthermore, children who remain "typical" viewers from the age of three through seventeen will end up spending more time in front of the television set than in school.

Many experiments have been conducted across the country to determine the effect of TV on children who watch it from twenty to twenty-five hours a week. On the positive side are the suggestions that TV broadens a child's vocabulary and increases his awareness of the world around him. However, the electronic baby-sitter results in young children watching far too much television and certainly some wrong programs.

Dr. William Glasser, educator, psychiatrist and director of the Los Angeles center for training teachers in reality therapy, advocates that TV limits the growth of a child's brain capacity and may interfere with his creativity and curiosity. He recommends that children up to 10 years of age should be limited to one hour of TV a day.

One young mother tells the story about how she was in the habit of keeping the TV set on all day long. She didn't really watch it but just had it on for company. Her sixteen-month old baby was a perfectly healthy child except that he slept rather restlessly and was crankier than most babies. She decided one day to turn off the TV and not play it for long hours as she usually had. It had never occurred to her that there was any connection between the TV and her child's restlessness, but the child's behavior changed quickly. He began to sleep better, he could concentrate on his own child's play much better, and he was much more contented. One psychologist says, "television is too much noise, too much stimulation, and too much syncopation for a young child even if he is not watching."

Educators have been noticing a changing pattern of behavior in children and they are attributing it to television. A school teacher commented that one little child had never walked normally at school. Every motion was exaggerated and slow moving, an imitation of the "Six-Million Dollar Man." The veteran teacher reported that there is an increase in children's shyness, passive behavior, and withdrawal, and they exhibit less creativity, imagination, or active involvement.

Too much television robs a child of the enjoyment of good books. TV will never be an adequate substitute for the world of adventure found in children's books. I have reported these findings that show that TV may be hindering your child's intellectual development for your information, but I do not mean to say that TV should be an absolute taboo, not at all. However, it is important to guard what he watches and limit his time. Even too much good TV time can hinder your child's individual creativity. Four is the age to put limits on TV time before he establishes a pattern that is hard to break later on.

The choleric child will probably not be interested in too much TV. After all, it isn't productive. Choleric children hardly like to play with toys. Little sanguines will probably watch more TV but will want someone to watch it with them. They will wander in and out from the TV room to the cookie jar. Most TV watching will be done by the melancholic who will lose himself in what he watches and take the TV program very seriously. The phlegmatic will watch TV and will sit glued to it until he falls asleep on the floor. Childish temperaments are unstable so these TV reactions are not absolute, but they may help you to be alert to the possible effects of TV and the dangers to your child.

E. SPIRITUAL DEVELOPMENT. A child of this age needs to learn that God made everything around him—his lovable kitten, the delicious bananas, the cold water, and the beautiful flowers. As he becomes aware of things around him he will realize that all good things come from God.

Some children become alert to spiritual matters more rapidly than others and begin to ask questions that could lead to their salvation very early. One of our daughters during this period had the traumatic experience of seeing her dog run over by a car. She began to question us if her doggy had gone to doggy heaven. We satisfied her by saying that God certainly must have a place for dogs of little girls. Then she asked if she would go to heaven when she died. Very simply we explained to her that she would, but first she would have to invite Jesus into her heart. She responded, "I want to invite Jesus in right now." We all prayed and I firmly believe that on that day, at four years of age, she was saved.

Today she relates back to that day as the time of her salvation. However, not every child will make a decision for Christ at that early age. It is important that you just take each day a step at a time in leading your child to a vital relationship with Christ.

F. BOOKS. Again I would like to stress the great value that books play in your child's life. Research studies have shown that the extent a child is read to during these early years correlates highly with his success in school. The preschooler needs to be read both fiction and non-fiction. Fiction increases his imagination and his creative thinking; non-fiction gives him basic concepts that help him to understand his world and God.

A few books are listed below that I consider excellent material to be read to your child. Please examine them first to be certain they are suitable for him. This is a mere sampling of the vast array of books that are available. I suggest you visit your neighborhood library and your local Bible bookstore for a more complete list of books available.

Series of *I Can Read* books, (Harper).
A Hole is to Dig, Ruth Krauss, (Harper).
The Mr. Small Books, Lois Lenski, (Walck).
Horton Hatches an Egg and others by Dr. Seuss, (Random).
Fairest Lord Jesus, Frances King Andrews, (Broadman).
Everywhere I Go, Dorothy Andrews, (Christian Literature Crusade).
Little Visits with God, Jahsmann and Simon, (Concordia).

G. CONCLUSION. This, by no means, has been an exhaustive discussion of the four-year-old. It was intended to serve as an additional aid and encouragement to what you are already doing right. These should be happy days for both parents and child, and if you follow sound, basic Biblical principles for training, then this fourth year can well be a giant step in establishing stable parent-child relationships.

By now you have seen definite progress in his life from a totally helpless infant to a youngster whose foundation is well established for becoming a responsible adult. A good motto for the parents of four-year-olds should be: "Never do for your child what he can do for himself." Remember at the end of this stage you will have helped him develop 50 percent of the intellectual potential he will ever have.

6

Sandbox, Skinned Knees, And School Days

From this point on children advance more individually and there will be overlapping of characteristics plus indefinite boundaries on different events in a child's life. In spite of this I have proceeded to place assorted topics in the general areas where you are most apt to meet them. I am counting on moms and dads being flexible and not holding me to too rigid a time schedule.

A. SCHOOL DAYS. Sometimes Christian parents are only concerned that their children invite Jesus Christ into their life and overlook the detrimental influence that a secular education can have on their child. Too many children have been lovingly led to Christ at their parent's knee and then thrown to the destruction of the public school system. Wise parents will investigate the schools in their area. Talk to the teachers and the principal, look at the textbooks, and even visit a few classes in different grade levels. If you live in a city where there is no choice of schools, then your job at home takes on greater dimensions as you seek to counteract any negative influences that the school might have on your child. You should be aware that not all Christian schools meet satisfactory standards, just as all public schools do not. But today, many Christian schools have improved to such a degree that they stand head and shoulders above public schools. Each one merits your investigation. In the long run, however, I would rather take the chance and send my child to a Christian school and have to enrich his training at home than to send him to a public school and try to undo much of the wrong influence received there.

I greatly appreciate the illustration given by Kenneth and Elizabeth Gangel in their book, *Between Parent and Child*. They state that there are three influences on a child's life during the approximately 100 waking hours in a week. They are divided as follows:

School takes 35 to 40 hours a week.

Church and related ministries add 5 to 6 hours a week.

Home and parents have the remaining hours.

The school occupies almost half of his waking hours each week. When all three of these influences agree on values and truths, they cooperate together in training the child. When one area of the three influences presents opposing or contradictory views, then the other two must compensate and produce corrective training to counteract that portion.

Why do I present this subject at such a young stage? Because the time to start the proper training is at the very beginning when he is most impressionistic and easily influenced.

This is the time when many mothers go through an emotional shake-up as they realize their little darling is about to break out into the cruel world and that never again will there be the uninterrupted relationship between mother and child. Not only will she be sharing her child with a teacher who will greatly influence his life, but he will be gone from her care for as many as 20 to 30 hours a week. No wonder many a mother sheds a few tears on that first day of school when he leaves so excitedly to conquer his new world. Then the shock is almost too great when one day he challenges his parent's authority by saying, "But my teacher said this is the way to do it."

Some children develop real anxieties about separating from their mother and are afraid to start school. They may be eager when they leave the house, but by the time they get to school they are afraid because the teacher and the other children are strangers. This may cause him to shrink back when the parent leaves him at the door of the school and he may cling to Mom's legs for security. There have been some very unpleasant and highly emotional scenes at the front doors of many schools.

Most schools try to minimize this anxiety by inviting the child and parent to visit the school together before the child is left there alone. However, the way to prepare the child to face this separation from home is a sensible attitude by the parents that prepares for that first day. A child that has started off as an infant attending the church nursery will be three steps ahead of a child who has never been left in a nursery. He has become familiar with the procedure that after a short separation from Mom and Dad, they always show up to claim him again. Young children who have been used to going out in public or having an occasional baby-sitter will be better able to adjust to opening day of school.

The parent should never appear to be embarrassed, agitated, or angry regardless of how much commotion is made on the first day. It is a mistake for a parent to wait until the child is absorbed in play and then pull a disappearing act. The anxious child will conclude from this that the parent cannot be trusted. The wise response would be for the parent to instruct their child that everybody who starts school keeps going until he is finished.

Some mothers have suggested that it was easier for their child to leave them than for them to leave their child. If this is a possibility, you might prearrange with a high-school-aged friend to walk with him to school the first few days. That way he has left you at home; you have not left him at school.

You can probably expect that the phlegmatic child will have the most difficult time making the break from home and adjusting to a new, strange surrounding unless the parent has done a successful job of preparing him. He is just naturally more fearful anyway and will need the extra time required to prepare for that first day of school.

The sanguine will be fine the minute he arrives and sees other children at school. Any fears he might have had will be immediately dismissed. In fact, he will probably be the one to comfort other fearful children who are hesitant to enter into the activities.

It will not be hard to spot the choleric child on opening day.

He will be there to give directions on what door to enter and be in full command of the slide or other playground equipment. Fear is not a part of his temperament. He knows that school is something you have to do so you might as well do it.

The melancholic will be slow to get involved in the group activities. He will be a little suspicious and may question if his mother is going to pick him up after school. His attention most likely will be drawn to something he can do quietly and all by himself. His mental attitude has to be prepared to help him want to go to school.

One of our children went through a difficult time when he started school. We had prepared him for months ahead to look forward to the beginning of school, and he did very well adjusting to the first three weeks. He would leave happily every day for school and come home expressing his delight in his teacher and new friends. However, after the first three weeks our family had to move, and he not only moved to a new home and new city, but to a new school. All the preparation we had built into him was of no avail. It was traumatic for him and for us, but with much love and security poured upon him, he gradually overcame it. Today he is a grown man and has developed into a very normal adult.

On the bright side, the distress that a child experiences at the beginning of school, even though it might be troublesome, is a very normal occurrence and does not indicate a disturbed child.

B. MENTAL GROWTH. It is very exciting when the first grader begins to recognize words and develops a real feeling of accomplishment. When he is in the third grade he will have developed a wider vocabulary and will be able to read aloud for others.

The academic accomplishments during these years are fantastic. He will move from very little knowledge to a working knowledge about math, reading, writing, science and spelling. He is full of curiosity and enthusiasm for learning. Remember, 80 percent of his capacity for learning will have been developed by the time he is eight years old. Expose him to many opportunities for learning. He is very responsive to intellectual stimulation and should be challenged and stimulated to increase his capacity. Don't underestimate his capabilities!

C. PHYSICAL GROWTH. This primary child has gained more poise and muscular skills. He desires to do things instead of watching others do them. Don't expect him to sit still very long. His interest span is still rather limited. His muscles seem to tire when he is in one position too long and this causes him to wiggle and squirm. He is young and active, but he tires easily; therefore, he should be in bed at an early hour in order to get sufficient rest.

His television viewing should not be made up of violence or frightening programs which would cause him to have nightmares or restless nights. In fact, the less TV he watches, the better he will be able to completely relax in his bed.

He seems to have spurts of growth. The most common remark from mothers of this age is that they can't keep them in shoes or clothes because of their rapid growth. His greatest growth is in his arms and legs, which makes him taller and thinner.

Their most frequent trademark is their toothless grin and uneven teeth. Large teeth will be growing next to small teeth. It is very obvious that he has come a long way during these few years.

D. SPIRITUAL GROWTH. This child has a rapidly growing concept of God and may be ready to accept Christ as his Saviour. The parent should be sensitive to the questions he asks concerning God, heaven, death or sin. Be careful not to force the child to make a decision about something he does not understand. Not all children at this age are ready to receive Christ. In this case, continue leading him to understand more about God and Jesus. However, if you feel that he is ready and understands what he is doing, then by all means lead him to invite Jesus into his heart. He must understand that it is only because of God's love that he can be forgiven of his sins.

He usually loves Sunday School and looks forward to Sundays as the best day of the week. However, the attitude that the parents have towards Sunday School and church will gradually be adopted by the child, whether it be positive or negative. His mind should be challenged to memorize Bible verses, but they should be verses that he can understand and can translate into everyday experience.

E. SPECIAL TRAINING. There are several areas where a child needs special training during this stage. One is training in basic social behaviors. Young children are not automatically courteous. This comes only by training. They want everyone to listen to them when they want to talk, but with training they will learn courtesy in listening to others. The three important words to stress at this age are "please," "thank you" and "excuse me."

The most effective training is through practicing politeness and respect in the home. When the parent and child make a habit of courteous habits at home, then it is much easier for both of you to behave in this manner in other situations.

He has to be continually helped to share his own possessions since he may tend to be selfish. He needs to learn how to "give and take." Even though he may have a temperament that is naturally generous, he will tend to go through a stage of selfishness at this time. He is still the center of his own universe, and he needs to be taught that he cannot always be first or have the most or the best.

Temper tantrums are usually over by this age. But, if he is a sanguine or melancholic, he may occasionally lose his temper. The child who responds to punishment with an angry explosion definitely needs some strong measures of discipline. Probably the most frequently asked question in our seminars is, "What do you do with a little child that cries out in anger after a spanking?" or as they say in South Africa, "after a hiding." After one seminar in South Africa, I had eight different sets of parents line up after the meeting to ask advice on how to cope with their child who responded to a "hiding" in a fit of anger. My answer for dealing with a child this age is to finish the spanking for the disobedience; then, when it is obvious that he is screaming in rage and not in hurt, go in to him and speak in a calm, medium voice. DO NOT BE ANGRY! Tell him that his punishment is over for the original disobedience and that you have forgiven him. And now you want to forget it. But his outburst is another problem that has to be dealt with. If you can say it honestly, then tell him that Mom and Dad do not burst out in anger like this and your home is going to be a place of peace and harmony. So the second spanking is for the fit of rage. It should be strong enough to send a signal to his brain that his outburst of anger is painful and will not be worth it the next time. This may have to be repeated many times, but eventually he will get the message that this anger is not acceptable.

When the anger is passed and the storm is over, it would be good to involve him in a discussion on what the Bible says about anger. Keep it simple so he can understand it, but he needs to know that you have the Word of God to back you up. It will be worthless to share this while he is in the midst of his rage. Proverbs 19:18-19 says, "Chasten thy son while there is hope, and let not thy soul spare for his crying. A man of great wrath shall suffer punishment: for if thou deliver him, yet thou must do it again."

Much of his behavior will be determined by what he thinks of himself. When a boy thinks he is "bad," he usually acts that way; or if a girl thinks she is "stupid," she will probably do things that make her appear stupid. It is important for parents to build up the child's self-esteem by refraining from ridiculing, criticizing or tearing him down. When he has done something that is worthy of an acceptable comment from you, be sure you give it. You build his self-acceptance and confidence by the way you let him know that you approve and accept him.

If your son or daughter still has problems with bed wetting, by all means do not punish or shame him. It is most likely that he is a sound sleeper and not aware of his impulses that tell him to go to the bathroom. He will be embarrassed and humiliated and will need your love instead of criticism and disapproval. Don't even show exasperation. Let him know that you fully understand and would like to make it a team effort to help him overcome this event in his life.

F. SPECIAL CHARACTERISTICS. This is the age in childhood where they like the opposite sex. Little boys will love little girls and they even decide which one they will marry when they grow up. A boy likes to talk about his girl friend at this age and even boast to others how many times he has kissed her. But as he becomes older, his talk will change because he does not want to be teased. He will think girls are "silly" and won't even sit next to them.

This is the age of meaningful questions. The best form of sex education is to answer the questions as they are asked. Answer them openly, directly, honestly, and matter-of-factly. If you avoid discussing these topics with your child, he can get the idea that you do not approve of this subject and it is "dirty" or "forbidden." You should be the one to inform him of the facts of life so be certain that the information is straight and that it is built around lessons on morality. Letha Scanzoni has an excellent book to assist parents in this important area of training entitled, *Sex is a Parent Affair*.

G. BOOKS. Perhaps by now you are receiving the message of what I am trying to say about books for your children. I trust you are already well established in the habit of reading together. As he develops in this stage, he will want to begin to read for himself. Encourage it. Go with him to the library, being careful that he does not bring home books that are too difficult for him to read. Our children were excited to read a book by themselves, but we still included the "reading together" time which involved several members of the family. In this way they were still able to exercise the adventure of books that were beyond their own reading skills.

You may begin to find that your child's response to listening or reading may be influenced by his temperament. The sanguine will want to flit from the first chapter to the last to quickly see how the story ends. He may tend to be restless and would rather be outside playing with his friends. Your encouragement will help keep him listening. You may find that he easily cries with sad stories and laughs at funny ones. The choleric would also rather be out playing ball instead of reading or listening. However, the kind of stories you select will keep his interest if they are packed with action and adventure. Once he learns to read, even a little, he would rather try to read by himself than be read to. It is the melancholic who will enjoy story time. He will probably want to sit right on top of you as you read to him and will become personally involved in each character. The phlegmatic will be willing to sit for long periods of time with a good book. If the story does not interest him, he will still sit quietly, but may slip off into daydreaming.

The range of books is very long, but I would like to list a few of our family's favorites. Any public library can aid you in checking out a regular supply of books.

Winnie the Pooh, A. A. Milne, (Dutton).

The House on Pooh Corner, A. A. Milne, (Dutton).

The Story of Ferdinand, Munro Leaf, (Viking).

Five Chinese Brothers, Claire H. Bishop, (Coward).

The Madeline book Series, Ludwig Bemelmans, (Viking).

Richard's Bible Story Book, (Zondervan).

Egermeier's Bible Story Book, (Moody Press).

It is vitally important for parents to be alert to their child's reading ability. Watch for the improvement of their skills. By the third grade he should be able to read smoothly with expression and comprehension. Ask him to read to you from time to time and show real interest in his achievement. It may be that he will need supplemental help during the first two years. If he does not learn to read well, it will limit what he can do for God in later years. Remember, you are what you read!

7

Multiplication Tables
To Skateboards
To Primping

The next few years will be characterized by an interesting conflict between fighting and loyalty to the gang, between hating the opposite sex and then primping for them, and between hating school and then enjoying it. These years are filled with energy, enthusiasm, arguing and learning.

Any parent with this age child will enjoy their junior boy or girl more if they will learn to relax and laugh with or at them occasionally. Be careful not to turn him into a complex human being. If you have already determined his temperament, it will help you to understand why her room is always messy, why he spends so much time in the principal's office, why she has scraps with her best girl friends, or why he wears his good pants to play football. How you learn to enjoy and guide them in the midst of these extremities and aggravations will determine a great deal how you will relate to them as teenagers. Be an encouragement to them and build them up. You will be building on the foundation that you laid a few years back.

A. LEARNING—BURDEN OR BENEFIT? School is a necessity but can be such a burden to some juniors. The temperament will play an important role in his attitude toward school. When the school bell rings at the close of the day, there will be some students who will race out the door like the building was on fire, while others will linger long after school is dismissed.

The sanguine and choleric will knock each other over getting out the door. In fact, they will probably be out of the building before the bell has stopped ringing. It's not that they are so eager to get home to their mother, but that they are both lovers of sports and competition and can hardly wait to reach the playground after school. The sanguine will enjoy any activity of play as long as there are other kids around. When they start to leave, he will too. But the choleric will be the last to leave, especially if there are organized activities. He has a driving compulsion to be a winner and will want to play longer to get a chance to win or to win again. Neither of these temperaments are too concerned about tomorrow's homework assignment.

The melancholic will linger after the bell for many reasons. For one, it is highly possible that he or she will be infatuated with the teacher and will want to stay longer to help and be near her. He is eager to wash blackboards, clean erasers, or any number of other things. There is also the concern that he might forget an assignment, so he finds it necessary to go over all this with the teacher again. And, of course, he will take every book home just to be sure he has the right one.

The slowest one to leave may be the phlegmatic. He will start to clean out his desk after the bell has rung. His desk will be straightened and reorganized over and over again. Then when he finally leaves school he will poke all the way home. He will kick every pebble and pet every dog and cat. When he finally arrives home he remembers that he forgot to bring his assignment with him.

Regardless of his attitude to get out of school at the end of the day, every child at this age should be stimulated to study and to think. He should be challenged to do some real thinking. When he asks questions, it will be most beneficial if the parent would guide his thinking so he can discover the answer for himself rather than just give him the answer. Help him to establish good study habits, especially the sanguine or phlegmatic who will tend to procrastinate and dilly-dally around. Provide him with an atmosphere and the equipment for study. When the TV is blaring and the family is yelling across the house, it is difficult for any human being to study. Parents should never do the work for the child, but should show a genuine interest in the homework and be able to discuss it together. The child will be impressed and challenged when the parent is interested in what he is studying.

Most boys and girls of this age love to read, and the wise parent will encourage it. He will enter this stage as a slow reader, but his reading skills should develop rapidly which will enable him to read with speed and comprehension. Any encouragement the parent can give to better the reading skills will benefit the child for the rest of his life.

We were fortunate to live close to a public library during these crucial years in our children's lives. This library ran a three-month summer reading program for the neighborhood kids. It was very competitive and junior boys and girls love competition, whether it is in sports or reading. A large chart was posted inside the library door with the name of every kid who entered the reading program, and each week the number of books he finished was posted for all the world to see. The program required that each competitor read at least two books a week to stay in the competition, and they had designed a clever way to determine if the child had read the book and understood it. One summer our children read so many books that I finally had to limit the amount of time each day they could read in order to keep a proper balance. But their reading skills and vocabularies increased with great strides. It is important that the child at this age does not read to escape reality. If he feels inferior to his playmates, he may retreat to the security of a book. Thus, it is wise to keep a good balance for his proper development.

Reading opens up new areas of interest also. Reading helps boys and girls become more interested and informed in science, famous people, history, geography, Bible stories, etc. Books will help to broaden the horizons of each young reader. I firmly believe that books become more interesting to any child when the TV is limited in the home. Books and TV mix about as well as oil and water. Good books will stimulate any person's imagination and creative abilities.

There are many good books that juniors should be familiar

with. In fact, there are so many that it is virtually impossible to begin to accumulate a list for them to read. A reliable list of excellent books for all ages is found in Gladys Hunt's book, *Honey for a Child's Heart* (Zondervan). It is a guidebook for both secular and Christian books for parents to consult regarding reading material for each age. Probably at the head of any list would be the seven children's books by C. S. Lewis; the first of the series is titled, *The Lion, The Witch, and The Wardrobe*.

B. ENERGY FOR PLAY BUT NOT FOR WORK. Unfortunately energy is wasted on the youth and all he wants to do with it is play. How often adults wish that they could bottle up some of this boundless energy for the more productive years. The junior boy or girl can work very hard at playing, but he hates it if you ask him to work. I watched several boys "play" very hard to clear a portion of snow off the ice for skating. If their fathers had asked them to shovel the snow off the sidewalk, that would have been called "work" and they would have hated it. They are full of energy and need direction and guidance to be certain their energy is used constructively and not destructively. It is remarkable how quickly their zeal fades when asked to do the dinner dishes. Subtle motivation may stimulate them to get the job done and then do something that they find more enjoyable, such as making a suggestion, "After we are finished with the dishes I will challenge you to a game of twenty-questions" (or whatever the family game is at your house). Give them a goal to reach beyond the unpleasant task they must do.

C. SIN IS SIN. This child is now old enough to recognize that sin is sin and will feel the guilt that it produces. Some children have already received Christ by the time they enter the fourth grade, but statistics show that more people accept Christ during these years than at any other time in life. Their hearts are ready and they sense the need for help to overcome their temptations. If Mom and Dad have laid the proper groundwork during the previous stage, then it should be very normal for him to receive Christ during this period of life. But again, the parents' attitude toward Sunday School, church, and Jesus Christ during his junior years will be reflected by him when he reaches junior high. When a parent stays home from church every time a "Sunday headache" occurs or his favorite team is playing football on TV, the junior boy or girl will begin to capture the same spirit.

Since this is such an important stage in the spiritual life of a young person, it is very vital that the Sunday School give it the very best. The most capable and Spirit-filled leader in the Sunday School should be in charge of the Junior Department. Dr. Henrietta Mears once said that a junior should not be graduated out of the department without receiving Christ. Every teacher in this department should be committed to this goal. Woe unto the teacher who is careless and negligent to pray and prepare for that important hour each week that they have to influence a junior's life.

The child's education regarding Jesus Christ and the Christian life can best be done in the home and should be started at an early age. Then it becomes a normal acceptance of spiritual concepts and he adapts them to his own life. Your prayers and faithful teaching, including his Sunday School training, will lead him to an acceptance of Jesus Christ as Savior.

D. FAMILY WORSHIP. Family worship is a very valuable part of training the children, but in too many homes it has become a very formal and stiff period of time after the evening meal that the whole family looks at with boredom. There is nothing spiritual in sounding the gong and announcing that "family worship will now begin." Since the Bible does not tell us how family training should be accomplished, why not use a little imagination and give it variety and interest? May I suggest that the family devotions be a very natural and informal time with everybody participating. Does it have to be after the meal each time? Let it be a planned discussion during the meal that is instigated by Dad with everyone participating, and then Dad concludes with God's words. This can be practical, interesting and geared to any age level. The junior boy or girl especially enjoys this type because it is not all listening and he can be involved in it, too. This can be a great time for teaching practical Christian living to your children.

E. SPECIAL CHARACTERISTICS. The junior child usually feels rather awkward about an open display of affection. They want to be loved and need to be loved, but don't overdo it, especially with the boys. When Aunt Mathilda comes to visit and plants a big kiss and hug on junior, it causes him to do all sorts of funny things. We had one son who seemed to disappear when certain people came to visit. He could not handle any outward show of affection to him at this stage in life. Rather than make him stand there and allow Aunt Mathilda to embarrass and humiliate him, treat it nonchalantly. If he chooses to disappear for awhile, don't go in and drag him out. Sooner or later he will slip back into the room unnoticed and blend into the family activities. Forcing him to react contrary to his emotions will only make a bigger issue of it than necessary. Moms and dads should still display love and affection to their junior son, but do it discreetly. Don't insist on kissing him good-bye in front of the school when you drop him off some morning. Keep your kisses for that goodnight hug in the privacy of his bedroom. My husband would faithfully go into the bedroom of our sons, pull the covers around their neck, and tell them that he loved them as he tenderly placed a goodnight kiss on their head or cheek. But outside in public they seemed to understand each other and good-bye was just a touch on the shoulder or a pat on the back.

Girls do not seem to struggle with this as much as boys. Our girls seemed to be better able to cope with love and affection in public. Here again the temperament plays an important role in how your daughter responds to affection, as does the foundation you have laid prior to this age. Every girl needs to feel free to sit on her father's lap and put her arms around his neck. This is the best preparation a girl can have for becoming a responsive, loving wife. If a junior girl does not have a warm, open relationship with her father, then it will be difficult for her to have a loving relationship with a marriage partner.

Junior boys usually think girls are "silly" and "stupid," and junior girls think boys are "show offs" and "pests." For many years I was in charge of the junior department in our Sunday

School. One absolute distinctive characteristic I noticed was that junior boys did not want to sit in the same row with junior girls and vice versa. In fact, the greatest competition and friendly rivalry in contests and Bible drills came from putting boys on one team and girls on the other.

Dislike of the opposite sex promotes a greater spirit of love for the "gang," particularly with boys. They like to do things in a bunch rather than singularly. There is a real spirit of loyalty between boys that are in the same gang—more so than with girls. Girls at this age don't seem to get along too well together. They will sometimes even pick a fight with their best friends.

It is wise for the parent to be observant but not involved in these girlish skirmishes, unless the situation gets out of hand. Usually the girl she fought with last week will become her bosom buddy within a few days. The choleric and melancholic girls are most likely to be disagreeable with their best friends.

The demand for fairness is a natural characteristic of a junior child. If something appears to be off-sided, he will quickly respond with "That's not fair." He recognizes injustice, so be ready and willing to admit it when you have dealt with him unfairly. Ask his forgiveness. Years ago my husband had punished one of our sons for a deed and then it became apparent that he had punished the wrong son. When a parent realizes this, he must be willing to confess the wrong to the child and ask his forgiveness. It isn't enough to just say, "Well that serves him right for all the times he should have been punished and wasn't." My husband admitted his wrong to the boy and asked his forgiveness. Our son looked his dad square in the eye and said, "Of course, Dad, I realize that you are not perfect!" They know we are not perfect parents anyway, so why try to bluff them. Many years later while speaking at a Family Life Seminar, I told this story and our son, now grown and the father of two boys, was present in the meeting. Afterwards he said to us, "Dad, that's strange. I don't remember that spanking you gave me." My husband turned to me and said, "Honey, you can be sure he would have remembered it if I had not asked his forgiveness." How valuable it is to deal fairly, squarely and honestly with our children.

Very few junior boys or girls care how they look. Their hair can be tousled, shoes unlaced, shirt or blouse hanging out, or dirt smudges where they have wiped their hands on their clothes. Their shirt can be dirty and wrinkled, but if it is their favorite, they will want to wear it again. Perhaps the phlegmatic will be an exception to this because they are basically neat and tidy. However, at this age even they can be different. They all need to be encouraged to care for their own belongings and to have a neat appearance. A junior's room is usually a disaster area if left alone. One parent related the story to me about their daughter. Her room was continuously in a disorganized mess and clothes would be generally left just where she took them off. One evening when everyone was away, their burglar alarm sounded and the police arrived. Moments later, the college-age son came home and found the police walking around the outside of the house. They quickly explained that the alarm had sounded and one policeman said, "I think I found the room where they entered. It looks like it has been ransacked. The policeman led them around to the window of the girl's room and they all peered in. Sure enough, it did look like it had been ransacked, but the son said, "No, her room always looks like that!" It was a false alarm and the officers went away chuckling to themselves.

This is an area where parents need to motivate and encourage their children to improve. Nagging will not do it! It will take teamwork between parent and child to get him going and help him know how to do it. He will generally want to do it by himself, but if he knows that you are going to come and assist him, that will usually motivate him to clean up his own mess.

At the close of this stage you will begin to see traces of change appearing. The boys will start to linger a little longer in front of the mirror. Girls will take a little more care to see that their hair is curled and their clothes are looking just right. And one day soon you will wake up to the fact that the bathroom mirror is always in use. It will either be the son primping or the daughter drying and curling her hair. What brought about the change? Sorry, Mom, you may think it was your excellent training, but it is simply that they have discovered the opposite sex in a new light.

F. HOW TO HANDLE MONEY. An integral part of a child's training is teaching him how to manage money. As he learns this, he will also be learning how to make judgments, accept the consequence of his judgments, and live with the problems he creates.

1. *Give him a regular allowance.* Set an exact amount (not too little or too much) that is paid once a week. Discuss with him what expenses his allowance is to cover. If he spends it all in one day and has to go without money for six days, he will quickly learn that it is wiser to spread it out over several days. Or, if he wants to purchase a more expensive item, he learns that he will have to plan and save for such things.

2. *Don't punish with money.* Money should not be confused with power or love. It is essential to keep praise and reproof separate from financial transactions.

3. *Let him make mistakes.* Spending money means making choices and everyone is bound to make a mistake from time to time. Don't automatically bail him out, but offer empathy and guidance. However, if he has really gone in over his head, you may need to extend him a loan that he will pay back to you from future allowances. But set it up in a business-like arrangement.

4. *Teach sensible saving.* Rather than encouraging him to save just for the sake of saving, suggest that he save toward a specific goal, such as a new bicycle. A junior will not be too excited about saving for a college education. That is too remote for him.

5. *Encourage him to tithe.* Regardless of how little the tithe might be, it is teaching a very valuable lesson to your child. When he learns to give 10 percent of his meager allowance to the Lord at this age, it becomes easier to give more as he grows older.

Each temperament will respond to money in different ways and the early allowance will help him profit from his mistakes. The sanguine will be an impulsive spender; the choleric will be the most practical with his money; the melancholic will be indecisive and, when he does spend his money, may have buyers' remorse; and the phlegmatic will be stingy and save it all for himself. It is good for the parent to observe how each one handles his money and then guide him to better management.

G. SEX EDUCATION. Even though a form of sex education has been going on for several years, your child is now approaching the age for more serious questions. If he is not asking any, it may be that he is getting his answers on the playground. In this case, the parent would be wise to naturally direct the conversation around to ask a few leading questions of his own. It is far better to have the straight facts from parents than to get the playground interpretation. A fine book for parents to share with their child when he reaches eleven or twelve is, *Almost Twelve*, by Kenneth Taylor (Tyndale Publishers). This book gives a simple but complete description of human reproduction as God designed it to be.

Too much information is more detrimental than too little at this age. Since they already have a dislike for the opposite sex, it is difficult for them to handle information that deals with too intimate a relationship. On the other hand, they need to learn the basics and have it interwoven with strong moral principles. Just before they enter junior high, it is wise for them to know that the pleasures of intercourse are not just for reproduction and that God has designed it to be reserved only for marriage.

H. CONCLUSION. This can be a fun age. They are now old enough to interact with you in conversation, work, or in playing games. This time will be what you make it. I have to chuckle inside when I hear my kids, who are now grown, tell others that we have always had a family tradition to do certain things. And they will proudly name several. Some of them I had forgotten about, and I didn't even realize others were traditions. But they have left impressions on our children, and now they are proudly labeled as "our family traditions." Families are drawn together in a beautiful unity by things that may be called "tradition" but really were created out of love and fellowship during this fun junior stage.

8

The Terrifying Tough And Tender Years

To a child there is nothing more exciting than his thirteenth birthday. (To his parents it is often terrifying!) This day signals his first step into the adult world. When he starts developing physically (if he hasn't already), he will accelerate the long process of becoming independent.

No other period of life is stormier than the teen years, not just for his parents but for the teen-ager himself. One minute he acts like a child, the next he feels like an adult. Cholerics want their independence before any other temperaments, then sanguines, melancholics, and finally the phlegmatics. As one authority said in pointing out the difference in teens, "Some thirteen-year-old girls are excellent baby-sitters, while others, at thirteen, still need a baby-sitter themselves."

At the entrance to the teen years, his sex is often more distinguishing than temperament. It is well known that girls tend to be more mature at this age than boys, not only physically but also mentally and emotionally. This accounts for girls' greater interest in the opposite sex and for their attraction to older boys. This differing maturation level usually evens out between 20 and 23. But don't expect a change in temperament; you will find that your teen-ager will manifest the same basic personality traits which he had when he was little, except now they take on larger and more adult proportions.

If you did your parental homework when your children were small, raising teen-agers can be real fun. But if you wasted the opportunities to mold their character and temperament when they were young, you will have your work cut out for you during the next six years of life. Dr. James Dobson, child psychologist, has aptly stated, "The time to disarm that teen-age time bomb is before he is five years old." A number of years ago, as my husband and I drove home after an evening of fellowship with friends whose preschool children sassed their parents and rebelliously threw their weight around most of the night, he remarked, "Those folks are going to have a heartache on their hands ten or twelve years from now." I am sorry to report that he was right.

Why All the Conflict?

Entrance into the teen years is not only exciting to the teen-ager, it can be downright terrifying at the same time. It means going to junior high school (where they start out on the bottom as a seventh grader after being a big shot sixth grader the year before) with new friends, new challenges, and new faces. In two years they may start dating, and in another year they go to high school and will even expect the keys to the family car. And in only six years they will either go away to college, enter the work force, or marry. In short, the prospects of adulthood can be frightening because it requires the one thing all human beings are most afraid of—change.

The most significant changes young teen-agers face are physical and sexual. The innocence of childhood is suddenly replaced by sexual feelings that inspire guilt. Girls often have amorous sensations causing the first boy-crazy stage that embarrasses both their parents and themselves. During a summer after graduating from sixth grade, one of our girls looked out the office window and recognized a budding ninth-grade girl friend she had long admired and said, "Ugh! I'm ashamed of Sarah. She is out there batting her eyelashes at the boys." Two years later I looked out the window to see our daughter doing exactly the same thing.

Fathers often forget and mothers cannot understand the trauma a boy feels when he experiences his first erection, or the shame and embarrassment he feels after his first nocturnal emission. The sanguine and choleric boy will find out from his peer what made him wake up "in a mess." The melancholic and phlegmatic will usually keep such experiences to themselves and carry unnecessary guilt for a protracted period of time.

Because of the guilt feelings associated with their emerging sex drives, don't be surprised if your teen-agers avoid showing affection to the parent of the opposite sex. This is usually a temporary period, but it is so important that they be assured of your love during that time. They don't feel worthy of your love, but want it and need it more than ever. Unfortunately, their behavior makes it difficult to love them—but love them anyway. The late Dr. Henrietta C. Mears, a great youth worker in her day, used to say, "At this stage of life only the parents can love them, and sometimes the father wonders how the mother can stand them."

Another reason for conflict is the intense feelings of inferiority and insecurity early teen-agers experience. As they enter this pre-adult world, they are usually unconscious of their ineptitude, inexperience, and insufficiency. Yet they have a real desire for acceptance. Consequently, they may act rebellious when you treat them like a child because they cannot perform tasks on an adult level. During this stage they need understanding, instruction, encouragement, but not constant criticism. Parental approval is worth more than we often realize.

When faced with this situation, try to avoid showing your exasperation when they foul things up. Remember what they were like just a couple of years before. They are certainly not mature yet, and it is unfair to expect performance beyond their capabilities. It is also important that you see your teen-ager as he is going to be someday: mature, dependable, and capable. If you think of him as inept, lazy, clumsy, etc., you will emote that message to him even if you don't say a word. That only confirms his feelings of inadequacy, particularly in the melancholic, the phlegmatic, and sometimes the sanguine youth. Keep in mind that the quest for recognition as a person grows every day after his thirteenth birthday. Your approval, whenever it is possible to give it honestly, will offer hope that he will someday make it. If you don't believe in him, he certainly isn't going to believe in himself. It is a known fact that the most important people in assisting an early teen-ager to accept himself are his parents.

Another thing that accelerates teen-age/parent conflicts all through these growing years is the teen-ager's desire for more freedom before their parents think they are ready. The parent feels, "Show me that you're responsible and I'll increase your privileges." The teen says, "Give me more privileges and I'll show you that I am responsible." One of the complaints I often hear from teen-agers is "My parents don't trust me." Yet often it isn't a matter of trust, it is immaturity. The teen-ager thinks he is more adult than do his mother and father. Most parents should give their teen-agers more adult responsibilities than they do, but it should be made clear that future opportunities depend on present performance. Parents have a right to expect their teen-ager to take reasonable care of his clothes, room, homework and other normal assignments in order to earn more adult privileges. It is impossible to give pat answers on when to "let go" and when to "hang on," but when a young person acts like an adult, he should be treated like one. Of course, the opposite is also true. The important factor is to be realistic in your expectations.

"The Four-F's"

To this day, our family (including those married and raising their own children) still refer to "the four-F's." It has always meant "family, fun, food and fellowship." Teen-agers often have lots of energy—except for work—and now that they are getting bigger, they can engage in more adult activities. Develop activities, hobbies, sports, etc., that you can enjoy together as a family. Take them on picnics, teach them games, and let them compete with you. It may take a lot of your time during a six- to twelve-year period of your life, depending on how many children you have, but it will save you heartaches later.

Today's life-style offers people more leisure time than any previous generation in the history of the world. Much of that time should be spent together, but you have to learn to do things that appeal to both teen-agers and adults. Sometimes that means teaching the young people something that you enjoy, and at times it may mean doing things to please them which may not be your favorite pastimes. When our children were young, my husband gave up golf for waterskiing with the family (he decided he didn't have time for both). In spite of the fact that at the time I was a nonswimmer, I learned to drive the boat because it was a "four-F's" event. Little did we realize we were gaining an activity that we could do together on vacations, even after grandchildren came along. (One requirement to marry into our family is the ability to water ski or a willingness to learn.)

Ever since I've known him, my husband has been a "football fanatic." Instead of fighting him over it, I decided to join him. Now I enjoy football almost as much as he does. When the children became teen-agers, we made a family event out of football. I prepared a picnic basket, and since we could only afford general admission tickets, we all went early, stood in line, and got good seats. Each game provided five to six hours of "family, fun, food and fellowship." The record book shows that the San Diego Chargers never did too well in the ratings, but our family scored high in family togetherness. Today we have holiday "four-F's" at our home throughout the TV football season. In addition to these activities, we have taken up snow skiing and other things. Little did we dream in those early days that our children would grow up to be our best friends.

Speaking of friends, all temperaments have friends, even the melancholic youth, although he usually doesn't have very many. One way to keep your children from running around with young people you don't approve of is to make your home a haven for their friends and let them invite them along on some of your "four-F" outings. Subconsciously they will select friends their family approves of. In fact, if your children are close enough in age, you won't have to say much when one invites someone who isn't a good influence on him; all his brothers and sisters will point it out—sometimes quite painfully.

Athletics As a Tool

Today's physical fitness craze has people jogging, cycling, climbing, snorkeling, hiking and a host of other things we never thought of as teens. Those who know say this craze is with us to stay, so you might as well use it as a tool. In their quest for personhood, it is important that your teens learn to do many things and that they do some things well. Every teen wants to be popular. Have you ever noticed that the kids who have many friends usually can do most anything, or because they do so many things, they are not afraid to try others? The girl that can bowl respectably, miniature golf without losing her ball, and play a decent game of tennis rarely lacks dates in high school. Boys today don't go much for wallflowers who are afraid to try something new. You may never be an expert at any of these things, but you can learn to enjoy them. And you can encourage your teens to learn. It is important for their development, as Dr. Dobson points out, that each child learn to excel at something. It helps him to gain much needed self-acceptance. Accomplishment in one area of life will give him confidence in others. Find out what your teen has an affinity for and get him to take lessons and practice consistently, if possible. If sports don't turn him on, try a musical instrument, band, hobbies or something else. They need to learn expertise in at least one area of life.

Unless your child is a natural born athlete (which can happen to any temperament), you will find his own temperament and his peer group will often determine his yen for sports. Sanguines are enthusiastic about everything, so they try their hand at every activity. Unfortunately their lack of discipline makes it difficult for them to keep at a sport after it loses its novelty, and their restlessness inspires them to try something else. Consequently, they often know how to do a lot of things, but nothing very well. Parental encouragement to keep at it during the drudgery stage, encountered in learning any sport, can well make the difference for the sanguine. The choleric child is a natural competitor and is often consumed by sports. He may letter in four sports and show little interest in dating or in scholastics all through high school. The phlegmatic youth needs constant encouragement to get involved with the other young people. He is not usually assertive and resists competition. Although well coordinated and basically capable, he rarely takes advantage of his potential. Once he gains confidence in his ability in a certain sport, he goes on to be above average. Phlegmatics are often drawn to the individual sports such as tennis, track or swimming. If, however, his peers are involved in a group sport, he may well put out the extra effort to excel in that also. Parental encouragement without nagging will make the difference.

Melancholic young people fall into one of two categories: either they are very good at sports and excelling comes easy for them or, more commonly, they show little or no interest or aptitude for sports. No one can be more anti-social than a melancholic. His talents are often in music, art, science or in the thinking fields. Such children should be started in sporting events early when they may find it less objectionable. If you've waited too long or they just are not interested, don't push them! It is important that you accept the cerebral loner or music lover for what he is. The world has benefited much from musicians and artists who had no interest whatsoever in athletics. But even so, learning to hit a softball, play volleyball, and swimming should be encouraged to enrich his church youth camp experiences and for his own physical well-being. Melancholic young people are often uncoordinated and find sports difficult. Since they take failure much more seriously than do the others, they will tend to withdraw rather than be publicly humiliated. Don't be deceived by their assertion, "I don't like sports," or "I can't do it." Many such children have benefited by loving parents who gave them enough backyard practice until they could play reasonably well.

Sports Aren't Everything!

You may think we are putting too much emphasis on

participation in sports. Some young people are just not well coordinated but can do other things easily. If that is true for your child, accept him as he is, find his area of talent, and help him to excel at it. But don't make the mistake of many parents who let the child's first feeble attempts discourage him so much that he quits. With encouragement he can find some sports that he can handle well. It will help him adjust to others his age and build his self-confidence. Besides, athletics are an excellent training ground for life. They require learning, practice, self-discipline, sacrifice and an ability to get along with other people. It has been my observation that by watching an athlete perform, you will find out what kind of person he is, for the pressure of competition reveals the participant's spirit. What he is on the playing field, he will be in life. If a child is selfish, dirty and unfair, it will surface on the playing field. If he is a griper or a quitter, sports will bring it out into the open so you can work on it. Years ago we had a sanguine-melancholic friend who was not well-coordinated and whose father, although a superb athlete himself, had neglected to train his son to be a good sportsman. Whenever he engaged in a sport he would inevitably cheat. When my husband used to come home from golfing with this man, he would grumble, "His best club was his pencil. He never adds all of his strokes." Years later his tendency to cheat surfaced and cost him dearly.

The Melancholic Loner

Parents of melancholic children are often disappointed to find that their son or daughter withdraws from others and enjoys isolating himself in his room to study, paint, listen to music, or work on some science project. The more gifted he is the more likely he will resort to such hermit-like behavior. It is so important that you use discretion with such a child! A sports-loving father (particularly a choleric and some sanguines) usually does everything wrong when this child resists athletics and withdraws from his peers. He may shame him, ridicule or coerce him, only to find he is driving him deeper into the cave of solitude. Once you have tried to bring him out, accept him for who and what he is. Then he can pursue his projects with your blessings and develop his native creativity and talents.

Young People and Their Church

Parents who take an active part in a Bible-believing church have a great advantage over an unchurched family when raising teens. The public school has turned into a zoo today. Drugs, immorality, pornography, violence, and in some places witchcraft, have replaced what once was a great educational system. Consequently, unless children are sent to a Christian school, which I advise wherever possible, the training they get in public school is likely to be opposite from what they need and what you desire for them. The church then becomes an ideal haven where they can be taught the principles of God for living and enjoy a social life that will reflect the standards of the home rather than undermine them.

Most progressive churches have a youth pastor or dedicated layman who plans an attractive junior high and high school program that will appeal to the average Christian teen-ager. At some time during these years, don't be surprised if your son or daughter becomes disenchanted with his youth group. Oftentimes parents blindly take the side of their teen when personality conflicts or personal jealousies flare up. To let them drop out of youth activities for such reasons sometimes can prove fatal! With four young people it seemed we usually had one that was displeased with his Sunday School class or youth group, but we insisted that he attend anyway and frequently found that before the year was out, he had changed his mind.

Christian parents would be advised to be supportive of their local church in front of their teens and insist on their active participation in everything their church offers for their age level. Don't be surprised if they announce, ''I'm not going to that church or youth group anymore!'' You are the parent, they are the children—your authority has now been challenged. If you tolerate this rebellion, non-Christian friends will take the place of their church friends and you will really have problems. Your church and its youth program are not perfect (don't expect them to be), but they are so much better than the alternatives that the question of whether they attend should not even be an option open to them. We found that the keys to the family car were all that it took to keep even our twelfth graders consistent when they didn't want to be. Young people, like children, will test your rules. Don't let their test catch you by surprise. Expect it and be ready with an answer.

Here's a suggestion to parents whose youth group is not all that it should be. We have found in our church that the problem is usually the lack of adult leadership. All Christian parents want a good youth program but few are willing to offer themselves to God to provide the leadership such a program requires. Years ago our youth pastor went against common practice and started challenging parents to work in the group where their teens attended. He wisely felt they had a natural interest in that group and should be most willing to sacrifice their time to make the youth program a success. At first the teens complained, "We can't get away from our parents." And some parents were afraid it would alienate them from their teens. Actually, quite the opposite happened. The young people and their parents had many interests in common and enjoyed doing things together; the kids became quite proud of the fact their parents were leaders or helpers. (Oh, they sometimes "bad-mouthed" the situation, but that was just meaningless talk.)

As we look back on the years with our young people, we treasure the church-sponsored outings, beach parties, river trips, camps, evangelistic outreaches, and other events we shared together. And we praise God for the vital contribution the church has made in each of their lives. One Sunday a nervous mother shook hands with my husband at the church door after the service and said, "Pastor, please pray for our family. We have three teen-agers all at the same time." On the way home he described her problem to me. "That woman is having all kinds of trouble with her teens and the only spiritual help they get is from attending Sunday School and church when they feel like it. They never come to the youth activities planned for them on Sunday nights or during the week." We had three teens at that same time, seventh through twelfth grades, but we loved it. One big difference was that our young people participated actively in all the youth activities, and most of the time, willingly. We praise God for the ministry that the church and its youth groups have had on the lives of our young people, as do many other parents who insisted their children participate. In many cases, those who refused to force their young people to attend have lived to regret it because their teen-agers took up with friends who were not Christians.

Screen Their Teen-age Friendships

Peer pressure is so powerful in the lives of teen-agers that at some stages in their development their friends have a greater influence on them than parents do. Between age fifteen and their senior year of high school (depending on their temperament), the influence of these friends can undo much of the good parents have trained into them. On the other hand, friends who are active Christian young people will fortify good family instructions and standards.

I Corinthians 15:33 contains some important instruction that often surprises many parents. For God says, "Be not deceived: evil companions corrupt good morals." We have seen unwise parents stand by and pray that their young people would discontinue a deep friendship with those of their own sex or the "steady" of the opposite sex that was having a bad influence on them. In reality, they were being derelict in their parental duties by not refusing to let them run around with those unsaved friends. As long as your children live in your home and eat your meals, you have the right to determine their friendships. The problem is, as even Dr. Benjamin Spock now admits, too many parents are afraid of their teen-agers' disapproval or fear the words, "I hate you!" It may surprise you that many teens in a fit of rage have said that to their parents, but it is a temporary feeling because they can't have their own way, particularly with friends of their choosing. At a time of spiritual carnality, you will find that the young people outside of the church will have much more of an attraction to teen-agers than the kids in church. The problem is not that the Christian kids are a "drag," it's that the worldly ways of your teen-ager's friends are more appealing to him because he himself isn't right spiritually. If you let him drop out of the youth group at church and run with the world, they will corrupt him.

My husband is in the ministry today because when he turned seventeen, his widowed mother found that verse in her devotions and realized his boyhood friends were turning him away from the Lord. She sat him down one Saturday morning and said, "Those boys are having a bad influence on your life, and I want you to break off with them and find your friends at church." Naturally, he refused! What carnal, self-willed teen-ager wouldn't? She then said, "Young man, you are too big for me to lick anymore, but I can't have your carnal life influence your brother and sister." Then through her tears she added, "As long as you park your feet under my table, you will do what I say; otherwise you will have to find another place to live." He was furious for weeks but finally he begrudgingly obeyed. Today he claims that as the turning point in his life. Personally, I thank God he had a mother like that!

Christian young people can help each other. All teens need someone in whom they can confide, particularly when they have a conflict with their parents. It is far better that they have a Christian friend who shares your basic convictions and who comes from a home where they have similar standards. Unsaved young people at a time like that will only feed their rebellion. Remember the Biblical principle, "A natural man does not accept the things of the Spirit of God; for they are foolishness to him, and he cannot understand them because they are spiritually appraised" (I Corinthians 2:14, NASB).

Guidelines for Dating

Dating is an exciting experience not only for the teen-ager but for the father and mother. Some parents say it is traumatic! Others find it an enjoyable part of raising their children. (But either way, you can expect your young people to date or wish they could.) As early as junior high, peer pressure for dating is a strong influence, particularly on girls.

The main cause for "trauma" during the dating stage of life is that it usually catches both the teen-ager and his parents unprepared. The young people have no idea what their parents expect of them, and the parents are not always in agreement with each other. That's a formula for disaster! We prepare our children for Sunday School, regular school, birthdays, Christmas, swimming lessons and almost every other event in life. Why not prepare them for dating? We found that if the first child is properly prepared, it is a relatively simple matter to get younger brothers and sisters to accept the same standards. If parents strike out with the first, they may also lose with the others.

Dating causes fear in many parents' heart for several reasons. First, it is a giant step towards independence. Parents don't usually accompany daters; consequently, they lose a large degree of control over them when they go out with someone else for two to four hours at a time. Second, some parents haven't learned to trust their children. Dating accentuates that lack of trust. Third, they have not prepared guidelines in advance; consequently, it exaggerates their fears.

We have had the privilege of using our guidelines for dating on ten children, four of our own plus six missionary children whose parents sent them to live with us for their junior or senior year of high school. Whenever we accepted teenagers of missionaries, it was with the proviso that they agreed to our dating guidelines. Although there were "confrontations" at times, both with the missionaries' young people and with our own, it was basically a very pleasurable experience. The following are the standards we have developed through the years.

1. *Dating is for fifteen-year-olds and over*. Reserving dating for fifteen-year-olds is no problem for boys. In fact, many of them are not interested until much later (or couldn't afford it even if they were). Girls are another matter! As we have seen, girls mature faster than boys both physically and socially. Consequently, they are often anxious to start dating very early.

Unfortunately, the boys their own age are often disinterested or do not appeal to the girls, so it is older boys that select the young girls and that presents its own problems.

Although fifteen is a recommended age to begin dating, that should not eliminate young people from enjoying each other's company at church youth group activities, camp or the like. But official dating, when a boy comes to a girl's home to take her on a specified outing, should be reserved until after that magic fifteenth birthday.

2. *Date only Christians!* One cardinal principle that is clearly specified in the Word of God is "be ye not unequally yoked together with unbelievers" (2 Corinthians 6:14). Dating is a yoke of fellowship that can someday be a prelude to marriage. The way to help your young people avoid the emotional trauma of ever having to decide "Should I marry this unsaved person with whom I am very much in love or should we break up?" is to refuse to let them go out with such an individual in the first place. It is very doubtful your son or daughter will ever get that involved with anyone they do not date. This standard may cause a few tears when they are forbidden to keep company with the handsome high school quarterback with whom they are infatuated, but it will eliminate a major trauma later.

Through the years we have watched fine, dedicated Christians, who dearly loved their children, lose them because they did not set this standard. I mention this here because we have recently had to pray and cry with several of them who lived to regret it. We know of two such girls, married at eighteen and divorced at nineteen. Needless to say, both the parents and their girls were brokenhearted.

3. *Schedule a pre-dating interview with Father.* When a young man dates your daughter, it is serious business because he is going out with one of your most treasured possessions. If a person borrowed your car or boat, you would clearly set some guidelines for its use. It is even more important when a young man goes out with your daughter. This may scare some prospects away, but you will find that is the group you want your daughter to avoid. Any boy who lacks the courage to look a girl's father in the eye when asking permission has no business

dating her anyway.

This interview gives Father the opportunity to do four things: One, to see for himself that the young man is really a Christian (hearsay testimonies aren't always valid). Two, to check his motivation. Does he have goals or plans for his life according to his age level or is your daughter his only objective for the moment? Three, to clearly lay down the guidelines they are to follow. Don't expect your daughter to do this. It is embarrassing for her. Besides, something might be missed in the transmission. Four, to size up the home life from which the lad comes. The answer to this question may not necessarily determine whether they can or cannot date, but if the young man loves and respects his parents, it helps you know what to expect in your relationships with him. The converse is also true.

When your son wants to date a Christian girl, it is somewhat easier for you to share with him your guidelines which are essentially the same as those for girls. He then sets the standards with the girl he goes out with. If he dates the same girl two or three times and you don't know her personally, you would be wise to have him bring her along to a "four-F" outing or set up an interview with both you and your partner. (The reason I suggest mother be in on this interview or get-together is because it is easy for a cute girl to "bamboozle" Father. It takes a woman to evaluate a woman, particularly where her son is involved.)

Bill Gothard did us and thousands of other parents a great favor in teaching at his seminars that guidelines for dating, including an interview with father, were very important. It really fortified our procedure and in recent years has made the process much easier for Christian young people to accept.

4. *All dates must be approved in advance.* Until young people get acquainted with you and your guidelines, don't let them stampede you into a quick approval of some type of activity which you do not favor. We made it clear to our teens that approved dating could include all church activities and outings, chaperoned parties, sports events, and special events they wished to request. The "don't bother to ask" list included movies, dances, unchaperoned private parties or any activity

where drinking took place.

5. *Until high school graduation, double dating only*. Probably the one standard the kids objected to most was double dating with another Christian couple. There is safety in numbers—not much, but some. The main reason for this, however, is to force them to make plans in advance and to avoid long periods of time when they can drift into "heavy couple talk." Under a wave of libido and the romance of the moment, it is easy to make premature love statements and commitments they don't really mean. The presence of another couple cuts down on this possibility drastically, even though it doesn't eliminate it entirely.

It is admittedly difficult sometimes to get up a double date, so to compensate for our stringent rules, we bent over backwards to make the family car available to our son whenever it was legitimate. Usually, if your son has the wheels, it isn't too hard for him to find a friend to double date with him—that is, if he really wants to.

6. *Absolutely no parking!* Mount Helix, (or the lover's vantage point in your city), may be a great place to park and "look over the lights of the city," but it is not too good an environment for avoiding youthful temptations. At this stage of life, touching the opposite sex is exciting, stimulating and dangerous. We believe dating is for fun and social fellowship, not to test their self-control.

One of our children testily said, "Dad, I get the feeling you don't trust us!" to which he replied, "You're right. I don't trust you, myself, or anyone else when they make provision for the flesh." You may ask, "Didn't your children ever park during their dating years?" We aren't so naive as to think they didn't, but if they did, we wanted it clearly understood it was against our rules. As one girl said, "Whenever I was tempted to park while on a date with a boy, I was always afraid my father might rise up out of the back seat."

7. *No undue public show of affection*. Love is beautiful to both teens and adults, but public demonstrations of affection that border on suggestiveness is harmful to the individual's testimony and may imply moral license to others. The Bible

teaches us to "avoid the very appearance of evil." The Christian community applauds teen-agers who obviously love each other but have enough self-respect not to maul each other in public. Proper dating should not detract from a young person's testimony or spiritual growth; besides, open expressions of affection today may prove embarrassing later when the interest in that person is gone.

8. *Curfew at 11:00 p.m. for girls—11:30 p.m. for boys* (with approved exceptions). Except for certain well-chaperoned functions we knew in advance would last later than 10:30 p.m., we expected our girls home at 11:00 and our boys at 11:30. (It took about that long to escort two girls, and another fellow home before meeting his curfew.) These early deadlines were universally resisted at first and were probably earlier than those set by most parents. Our reasoning was because there is very little wholesome activity going on in our city after 11:00 p.m. The good snack shops close then, and we think teen-agers should be home by that time. Admittedly most parents are more lenient. One of our daughters tearfully wailed, "Dad, I'm the only girl in the church that has to be in by 11:00." He lovingly reassured her, "I can't help it if the rest of the parents are wrong." Our son said after marriage, "One thing I found embarrassing about our family's dating rules was that all the girls I dated had a later curfew than I did." One girl asked him, "Larry, why are you bringing me home at 11:00? I don't have to be in until 12:00." In spite of the embarrassment and some problems, now that they are raised, we have no regrets. In fact, our daughter, who often chafed under the curfew, commented four months after the birth of her daughter, "Remember those dating rules? We're planning to use the same ones for Jenny when she's old enough to date!" (Life looks different when you are the parent.)

A problem for some parents may be how to enforce the curfew. Whatever hour you set for curfew will usually be considered too early and may be ignored. This creates much unnecessary conflict between parents and teens. We solved that very simply by clearly pointing out that every minute they were late coming home would cost them fifteen minutes shorter time on the next date. One lad brought our daughter home so late on a date that their next one was only one and one-half hours long. In fact, they had to quit miniature golfing on the seventh hole in order to make it home on time. But in four years of dating after that, they were only late once. Young people need to know that you keep your word, so they will probably test your rules. Be sure you don't flunk their test!

Many parents may think our guidelines are too stringent and decide to "massage these rules." Too often parents think, "I can trust my children," so they let them make their own dating standards or give them too much flexibility. Admittedly, in some cases it has worked very well, but in many others we have seen the good training of early childhood and adolescent years tragically marred by too much freedom in their teen years. Such parents have forgotten the powerful influence teen-agers have on each other and the tidal waves of libido that strike all normal young people. It is tragic when the self-control lessons of childhood are overpowered by these new and exciting drives they have at a time when they are least able to cope with them. In all of life these are the years of greatest emotional instability. It is so easy to make decisions on the basis of emotion rather than mind and will. Someone has said, "When the emotion and will are in conflict, the emotions invariably win." This is dangerous because emotionally-made decisions are almost always wrong. It takes a good deal of maturity for any person to learn that only when the mind and emotions agree is it right to proceed with anything. And even then the mind should be guided by the Word of God. Solomon said, "A wise son makes a father glad, but a foolish son is a grief to his mother" (Proverbs 10:1, NASB). That is also true of a daughter.

Respect the Rules of Others

You may not agree with the rules laid down by the parents of the young person your son or daughter dates, but if you can't respect their right to establish them, you had better urge your teen to date someone else. We were extremely fortunate with our eldest daughter in that the parents of the young man who is today her husband never encouraged him in objecting to our rules. Instead, they convinced him he had to respect our right to make them. When those two were married, the event also united two families. Now those young people are having a tremendous ministry with high schoolers and provide a good example of how Christian young people should face these tempestuous years.

Too Much Too Late

At our seminars many parents of teen-agers ask us, "How do you establish these rules when your young people are already dating on their own terms." The answer we give is, "Very gradually!" But be sure you do it. Prayerfully decide what rules you are going to establish, then sit down and very humbly admit to your son or daughter that you have been derelict in your parental responsibility and that for his and the family's good, you're going to establish some new guidelines for dating. Don't be surprised at the explosive reaction you get, but when the dust clears, you will have established a program that will guide your teen-ager in making some of the greatest decisions of his life.

When we planned a second Family Life Seminar in Houston, Texas, a man volunteered for the job of chairman. He is a successful businessman in that city and very active in his church. When asked why he was so enthusiastic about our returning there, he told us that he had attended our first seminar at a time when the oldest of his five sons was dating pretty much on any terms he chose. After hearing our guidelines, he went home and established a similar procedure. Although difficult at first, that decision had so changed his son and consequently, the atmosphere of their home life, he wanted other families in Houston to share the same opportunity for blessing.

After Graduation

The last big stage of teen training is their post high school years. It is during this time that they will be forced to make some of the greatest decisions of their life. Should they go to college or learn a skill? Where should they go to school or work? The answer to these questions will ultimately have a bearing on such decisions as what will be their life's vocation? Who will they marry? Where will they work and live? And where will they go to church? As you can see, these are momentous decisions and tend to chart the course of their whole life. Happy is the teen-ager whose relationship to his parents is such that they can serve as his counselors in making these decisions. The wise man of Proverbs said, "Without consultation, plans are frustrated, but with many counselors they succeed" (Proverbs 15:22, NASB). No one has the graduate's best interest at heart like his parents. So who is better qualified to be his counselors? But at this stage it will be received voluntarily or not at all. If you have not built the parent-counselor relationship between you and your child by graduation, it is very difficult to establish it in time for these vital years. But at least you can offer your suggestions.

Generally speaking (that is always a dangerous term), the Christian community has urged its young people to go to college as a means of increasing a young person's potential of service for the Lord. But the romance of "college after high school" that has dominated the post World War II years is coming to an end. Vocationally, there are many better paying jobs open to young people that provide a very constructive and challenging career. At one time it required a college education to get the best jobs, depending on his temperament and aptitudes. Today that is not necessarily true. However, academic training will give a young person more versatility for future areas of Christian service. One of the dangers of a secular college education today is that the whole educational system has been taken over by an atheistic, humanistic philosophy that is largely anti-God, anti-moral, and anti-American. Such a system seems to have a radical influence on the majority of students.

From my viewpoint as a Christian parent, and as the registrar for Christian Heritage College for over five years, I am convinced that all Christian young people should avoid the secular college as long as possible and trust God to provide them with a Christian college experience. In a Christian college or

Bible school they can best be trained to be the spiritual leaders of tomorrow, no matter what their ultimate vocation happens to be. Such schools give them an ideal environment in which to evaluate their vocational potential, to seek God's will for their lives, and to make friends with other Christians who are faced with the same decisions at this stage in life. Christian college professors will influence the young people spiritually whereas secular college professors often do just the opposite. The Christian environment also surrounds them with worthy companions while they are in the zenith of their emotionally combustible years. Those students who plan to go into medicine, law, science, or other fields that may require study at a secular college should consider one or two years first at a Christian college or Bible school to prepare them for the anti-Christian philosophy and environment they will ultimately encounter. The city in which we have ministered for over twenty years has seven secular colleges and universities. We have seen scores of fine Christian young people go down the drain or lose interest in spiritual things while attending such colleges. Many have married unsaved college companions and missed God's best for their lives. We have heard Christian parents say, "We can't afford to send our young people to a Christian college. We will send them to a state school; it is much cheaper!" It actually turns out to be the most expensive thing they ever did.

The real purpose for Christians having children is to bring them to adulthood to serve the Lord. To do so, they must study the Bible to become "approved unto God, a workman that needeth not to be ashamed, rightly dividing the word of truth" (2 Timothy 2:15). That doesn't mean that God wants all young people to be missionaries or ministers, but it does mean they can be trained to be Sunday School teachers, church leaders, office holders, youth workers, etc., for the rest of their life.

One of our dearest friends is a plastering contractor who had three years of Bible school training before he became an apprentice plasterer. During these thirty years he has held every office in the church, taught a Sunday School class, and led many to Christ. This man's parents feel that those three years in Bible school were a mighty good investment!

9

Training That Teaches The Total Child

I was standing at the nursery window of the hospital with my married son. His wife had just given birth to a tiny little boy. After several moments of silence where we both stood there in awe looking at this new little creature, Larry finally spoke. "Mother, it is my responsibility to train my little son in the way he should go. What does it really mean to train up a child?" He had asked a very profound question and I decided to find an adequate answer.

As the search began, I was not encouraged by some of the trite articles I read on training children. As a result of the varying backgrounds and priorities of each author, I found instructions on everything from toilet training to driving a car. That was not what I was looking for. I wanted to know what "training" really meant. What did God say about it? What did Proverbs 22:6 mean when it said, "Train up a child in the way he should go: and when he is old, he will not depart from it?"

The sermons and comments I had heard in the past led me to believe that if I trained my child in church attendance and if I lived a good example at home, that even though he might depart from it for a while, when he was old he would return to his childhood training. This left a sting in my heart and was not too encouraging. It was as if we could almost expect a child to depart from the faith for a period of time while he does his own thing. God forbid!

The best way to know what God means is to study His Word. After reading several translations and concordances, that verse took on a whole new meaning. I was so excited about what I had learned that I could hardly wait to share it with my son and to share it with all of you who may have been searching as I was.

The original Hebrew words shed new light on the verse, and with the risk of sounding heavy or cerebral, let me share these ideas with you in my own simplified manner.

Proverbs 22:6

1. "TRAIN UP"—The Hebrew word for this relates to the inside of the mouth—the gums, palate, or the roof of the mouth—and refers to the use of a bit or bridle that is placed in the mouth of an untamed horse. This is used to bring a wild horse into submission. James 3:3 (NASB) gives further explanation of the use of the bit: "Now if we put the bits into the horses' mouths so that they may obey us, we direct their entire body as well." It is necessary to train, or to bring the child into submission, in order that he will obey us, and thus turn about his whole direction. This is turning them from their own evil, selfish ways to obediently follow Jesus Christ.

2. "A CHILD"—The same Hebrew word that is used here for child is found several other places in the Bible. A few of these examples are:
   —I Samuel 4:21 is referring to a young infant that has just been born.
   —Genesis 21:14 uses this word when it refers to Ishmael, who was fifteen years old.
   —Genesis 37:30 makes reference to the child Joseph at seventeen years of age.
   —Genesis 34:5 is referring to Jacob's daughter who was of marriageable age.

The time span here for "a child" can be from infancy until the age when he leaves home to marry.

3. "IN THE WAY HE SHOULD GO"—This phrase more literally means "in keeping with his way" or "in accordance to the way he was designed by God." This does not necessarily

mean the way parents think he should go, but according to his own way, or simply the way for which he was designed by God. Parents must discover "his way" and adjust their training to it. The child's "way" may well refer to his temperament that was ordained by his Creator. Therefore, within the framework of the principles of God, train him according to his temperament or in keeping with his characteristics. We cannot train a sanguine the same as we would a phlegmatic or a choleric the same way as a melancholic. He must be trained in the way that God designed for him.

4. "AND WHEN HE IS OLD"—The word "old" here does not mean 60 or 70 years old! It refers to a male child when he begins to grow hair on his face or when he begins to enter the age of maturity.

5. "HE WILL NOT DEPART FROM IT"—What a thrilling promise! God has promised that a child will not depart from his parents' training if they have done what He asked them to do.

Did God Go Back On His Promise?

Immediately I can hear some parents crying out that they had given good training to their children, and yet they went their own rebellious ways. Therefore, God did not keep His promise. I would like to lovingly and prayerfully share some Biblical principles with you, so don't tune me out too soon.

First of all, some parents absolutely believe they have given their children proper training when they really do not have a right to claim this. It takes more than living a good example and taking them to church every Sunday. It takes more than loving and providing for them. One family comes to my mind that reveals this clearly. They were a beautiful family of four. The mother and father loved each other very much. They were patient, soft spoken, and kind to one another. Rarely a Sunday went by when they were not in church. But one important and tragic mistake was made. These fine people never insisted that their two children obey them, and the day came when the children followed their own desires instead of obeying their parents. Both of these children married unbelievers and are divorced today. They are not walking with God and the parents wonder why. Children have to be taught to obey their parents so they will obey God.

God's Requests	*God's Promise*
1. Bring your child under subjection	If we have fulfilled God's requests, our child will not depart from our training when he reaches maturity.
2. Teach him obedience	
3. Turn him from evil toward Jesus Christ	
4. Train him according to the way God designed him	
5. Train him from infancy to the time he leaves home to marry	

One of God's requests is training them to obey. When we fail to do that, then we cannot expect Him to keep His promise. Some parents have failed to bring their children into subjection while others have failed because they stopped the training too early in life or started too late.

What do parents do when they realize they are already negligent and time is swiftly passing? Perhaps their children are already grown and it seems hopeless that any changes can be made. There is hope because nothing is impossible with God. Consider the following steps, regardless of what stage your children are in, and trust God to bring about a change in their lives:

1. Recognize and admit the areas of your failure. Ask God to show you where you are weak and be willing to name the problems, i.e., pride, irritability, permissiveness, inconsistency, wrong priorities, etc.

2. Confess them before God and ask for His forgiveness.

3. Prayerfully and lovingly confess it to the family members you have offended and pray they will be forgiving.

4. Ask God to help you change your habits and develop a new plan to correct the old.

5. Have faith that the Holy Spirit will change your life and trust God to correct the wrong you have done to your children.

6. Begin living from this new point in life and not under the guilt of the past.

Keep in mind that your Heavenly Father is even more desirous than you are that you be a successful parent, but you do have to follow His principles. Parent, if you have sincerely followed the above six steps, then lift your head and enjoy life and your children. Don't be impatient for God to bring about a change! Love your children just as they are and wait patiently for God to work in their lives.

God Does Not Expect Perfect Parents

True, God does not expect perfect parents, but He has laid down for us a few basic requirements for training children. We can fall short in many areas, but God does expect us to train them in obedience and bring them into subjection.

Teaching obedience is more than giving instructions. It is instructing and then insisting on the child's compliance. Too often we tell the child what we want him to do, but we neglect to insist that he do it.

A terrific missionary, after twenty years of service, was passed over for leadership because of his refusal to carry out orders the way he had been instructed. After years of effective service as an assistant, although the heads of the organization loved and admired him and were fully aware of his great contribution to the work of the Lord, they could not trust him with complete control because he consistently refused to carefully follow instructions. He did not fight or argue but always did things "his own way." Somewhere, as a child, absolute obedience was not insisted upon. Consequently, he missed a great opportunity in life and had to go through an unnecessary and traumatic experience.

Effective training can be condensed down to a simple formula:

Instruction + Love + Insistence = **Effective Training**

Each step is an important ingredient in training and none can be omitted if we are to have the desired results. When instruction is given and followed by insistence to obey, it may well result in rebellion if love has been left out. Instruction and love are of little value when there is no insistence to comply to the instructions.

There really is no such thing as the "perfect" parent. And even if perfection could be reached, our children would not always be happy. You cannot judge the effectiveness of your training by the happiness of your children. With all your dedicated efforts to fill your children's lives with pleasure, each one will still experience many moments of real emotional pain that are necessary for growing up. Too often we are led to believe that we carry full responsibility for every phase of their emotional well-being. An unhappy child causes parents to feel guilty and to blame themselves. As each child goes through growth changes, there will be peaks of joy and depths of sadness, and neither can be counted on to last.

The most important challenge of being a parent is not to be perfect, but to teach the child to one day take full responsibility for his own life. The child enters the world totally helpless, so helpless that he cannot even scratch where he itches. And we as parents are to take that helpless infant to the place of complete responsibility during the course of 18 to 20 years. In order to meet that goal, it is necessary that the child experience for himself some of the emotional pains that are true to life so that he can grow into an authentic adult.

Teaching Your Child Right From Wrong

How do parents fail? When do children know right from wrong? Lying, stealing, cheating, breaking promises are all acts that even "good" children commit. Dr. Lawrence Kohlberg, professor of Education and Social Psychology at Harvard University, says children up to the age of ten rarely are capable of what most adults regard as "pure" moral judgments. Until at least that age, a child's notions of "morality" come, not from any abstract ideas of right and wrong, but from his feelings about what will happen to him. He obeys rules to avoid being punished, or he is "nice" to other people so that others will be "nice" to him. Children are born into this world with a dormant consciousness toward right and wrong. Too often an adult makes the error of assuming that a child understands the difference between right and wrong as an adult might. But children and adults think in very different ways. What matters to the young child is what actually happens, not the motivation behind the wrong act.

Very often we react emotionally to the things our children do, not because of the behavior itself, but because of what we read into it. When a child takes a toy from the dime store, we consider him a confirmed thief. When a little fellow strikes a smaller child, we see him as a lifelong bully. As our fears take over, we judge ourselves and then berate ourselves for having failed as parents. When we understand our children, we can be calmer—even as we make efforts to train and help them in their moral development. It is important to help him understand that God does not approve of stealing or hitting one another. But don't panic when he follows his sin nature. Instead, use that experience to train him that it was wrong, and that wrong actions must be corrected. First, he must correct it with God by confessing his sins, and then he must make restitution to the person he sinned against. This will produce a signal in him that he had better not do that again. A wrong deed is displeasing to God, Mom and Dad and, finally, to the victim of the circumstance.

The best time to teach and discuss morality is when a child has done something praiseworthy or when he is indecisive about a problem. It is very beneficial to the child to have to come to a decision by himself on certain issues. For example, Mary had promised to go over to Sally's house to spend the night. Sally had made great plans and was very elated over the upcoming occasion. However, another invitation was given to Mary to do something she liked even better and with friends she enjoyed even more. Now she was forced to make a decision.

Her parents granted her the right to decide but encouraged her to think about the moral issues in her dilemma. She was told she should do what was right; she should not let other people push her into a decision but should decide what things to consider to help make up her mind. Together they discussed who she had made a promise to. If that person trusted her to do what she said she would do, and if she breaks her promise and does something else, she would hurt that friend. She was told to consider how she would feel if she hurt her friend and how she would feel if someone broke a promise to her. She finally concluded that she would be too unhappy with herself if she broke her promise to Sally.

When using this teaching method, if you see that the child does not grasp the point you're trying to make, rephrase the problem and approach it at another level. Small children cannot see anyone's viewpoint but their own, and the ability to put oneself in another's place is essential to understand any issue that involves conflicting rights.

It is important to emphasize the concept of fairness. All morality boils down to the question of what is just and fair. God's standards for behavior are absolutely in line with this. Children develop a sensitivity of what is fair very early, even though its meaning changes as their skill in moral learning develops. Parents will also foster better attitudes in their children by avoiding such statements as "do it because I told you to." Instead, it is better to explain patiently the reasons for your rules and for their own beliefs and behavior. The authoritarian statement should be used only as a last resort when all the reasons and explanations have failed.

There are several methods of teaching the process of establishing values. One technique is called "values clarification." This technique has become popular because it is much like playing a game. This can be done around the dinner table, in the car, sitting around the fireplace, or anywhere the family is together. It is as simple as asking everyone a question such as, "What did you say or do this week that you feel God was pleased about?" One child may say that he had stuck up for a new kid on the playground when all the other kids were mean to him. Mother may say that she finished a household project that she had been working on for so long. Father may say that he confronted a man in the office with the fact that he continually used the Lord's name in vain. Another child may add that he had told a buddy how to receive Jesus into his heart. The conversation that follows seeks to sort out the values in each of their replies—loyalty to a friend and courage to go against the group, persistence in pursuit of a goal and setting priorities and allocating one's time, standing alone for one's spiritual convictions, and sharing with a friend a life-changing experience instead of keeping one's mouth shut.

Other questions may relate to how they would handle certain circumstances or how they would help a person in a given problem. Not only does this discussion pull values from each person but it also helps the children to realize that you respect their viewpoints equally with the adults in your family.

There is a great need in the home to create an atmosphere where everyone's dignity is respected and where everyone's thoughts are listened to and valued.

Don't Take Any Sass!

One mother's advice to her daughter when her first child was born was, "Don't take any sass!" This is a very simple, homespun philosophy, but that couple now has six beautiful, well-developed children that are a delight to their parents. This daughter taught her children respect by not permitting any sassiness or disrespect and entwining her correction and discipline with much love. A sassy child will not respect authority nor will he have a submissive spirit—both are essential to obedience.

Parents go through a great emotional shock with their first child. They bring that precious gift from God home from the hospital and that infant lies in his cradle looking like he has been carried to earth in the arms of angels. A beautiful picture to behold! Then suddenly, some nine or ten months later, that same angelic gift from God has the ability to curve his little rosebud lips and pronounce a distinct "no" in response to the parents' loving request. What a shock! I have seen young mothers cry with a broken heart when that little offspring stiffened his body and gave an emphatic "no" when he wanted his own way.

This is the beginning of several years of training that will determine the direction that child will go. When you begin by controlling his mouth, you will also begin to direct his entire body as well.

Society now has a generation of children raised in a spirit of permissiveness who have been allowed to act disrespectfully to their parents and others in authority. Is it any wonder that we are reaping the consequence of a generation of unbridled tongues? The young child who is permitted without correction to raise his fist in defiance to his parents will probably never be able to raise his face to Jesus Christ and say, "Dear Lord, what would you have me to do?" As James said, we need to put bits into the child's mouth so he will obey us and then we direct his whole body as well. The mouth reveals what is really in the heart. "For out of the abundance of the heart the mouth speaketh" (Matthew 12:34b). "But the things that proceed out of the mouth come from the heart, and those defile the man" (Matthew 15:18, NASB). The heart and the mouth are so closely related it is necessary to control the mouth in order to teach obedience and to train the whole body.

Are You Training Your Child to be Obnoxious?

Many moms and dads are training their children to be obnoxious! These well-meaning parents are certainly not aware of it, but the attention, approval and affection that a parent gives to a child are powerful tools in teaching this undesirable characteristic. Whenever a child's behavior causes a negative reaction from the parent, it will most likely be repeated. For instance, a child may ask for something in a normal speaking voice, but his mother doesn't respond. She is busy talking to a friend. The child's voice gets louder, shriller and more insistent. Finally, the mother pays attention. Unwittingly she has taught the child that the louder his voice and the more insistent he becomes, the more likely he is to get his way. The mother has followed a perfect formula for teaching the child to be obnoxious.

I once observed a father at mealtime who ignored his daughter when she quietly asked a question. The parent was engrossed in eating and a side conversation as the child continued to ask again. Finally, in desperation the child began to whine and carry on in an obnoxious manner. Now she had the father's undivided attention along with his irritable response.

Parents need to become aware of what types of behavior they are reinforcing in their children. Parents are a powerful influence in shaping good and bad behavior in their children by their well-planned or careless responses.

Children Have a Right to be Told "No"

Kids do not want everything they ask for. Many times they are asking for your help and are counting on you to say "no."

A young girl came home from school and announced that there was a new girl in her class. "She's really neat and her name is Barbara. She asked me if I could sleep at her house Friday night. I think maybe we could be best friends. Could I, Mom?"

Her mother glanced up from her newspaper, "Yes, dear, that will be fine," she said.

The young girl looked stricken. "I can?"

"I said 'yes,' dear; and don't forget to take your own hairbrush and comb."

"But, Mom," the bewildered, young girl said, "I hardly know her and I don't really want to sleep at her house. I would feel very uncomfortable."

The mother replied harshly, "You don't want to sleep at the new girl's house? Then why in the world did you ask me for permission?"

"Because Barbara invited me. I had to say I'd ask, but I was sure you would say 'no.' She's not really the kind of girl you would like."

Parents are many times tested and found wanting. The children may nag and coax, trying to wear a parent down and make him change his mind, but inwardly they experience real disappointment when Mom or Dad are not willing to stick with an original decision. One of the favorite remarks heard across the country is: "Everyone else gets to do it but me. I'm the only one who can't." This allegation is often a gross overstatement of fact designed to make the parents feel they are out of tune with the times. The best response to this is, "I don't care what the other kids are allowed to do. Their parents are responsible for them and I am responsible for you. God has given you to me to care for. The answer is 'no' and the subject is closed."

Children want to have well defined limits that clearly say "These are the boundaries. You may go so far and no further." All children are keenly aware that discipline is a special kind of love. It says to them, "I care especially for you. I will not let you get into trouble. My judgment is better than yours and you can trust me. I have been down that road and I know it well. You can rant and rave, call me 'square' and insist that I am an old fogy, but the answer is still 'no'—and it's final."

Your child will develop a sense of security and self-esteem when he realizes that you have firm convictions on certain issues and will not waiver when tested. Allow him to operate freely within the guidelines or boundaries that you establish for his good. The child that does not have these guidelines is the one who will undoubtedly suffer from a poor self-image and certainly a feeling of insecurity. He needs the assurance that somebody cares enough for him to give him a few definite rules for growing up in the right direction.

Parents, may God help you to be perceptive and do your children a favor by having the courage to say, "no!"

Respecting the Rights of Others

A giant leap toward reaching maturity is learning to respect the rights of other people. When a child learns how to esteem others' possessions, whether they be personal property or someone's time, he has learned a valuable lesson in becoming a well-adjusted and well-accepted human being. Probably the earliest beginning would be training a child to wait his turn to speak and not interrupt others when he gets a flash from his brain.

We were visiting in a home where there were young children. These kids could sit at the table with adults and behave superbly, except for one thing. When they received a sudden inspiration, no matter who was talking, they would immediately interrupt and demand that everyone at the table listen. One would not object to five or six interruptions, but it seemed as though the spurts of inspiration were coming faster and faster, and I suddenly realized that three or four of us at the table were left with a hanging sentence never finished. The mother merely commented on what quick minds her children had. Their tongues seemed to be quicker than their minds. I dare say that family has a problem. Those children did not respect the rights of anyone else at the table, nor will they ever unless they are taught soon to do so.

In contrast to this, my daughter gave me a beautiful example one time when we were visiting in her home. Her little four-year-old had something she wanted to say very urgently, but someone else was right in the middle of a story. My daughter leaned over and whispered to her that she would have the next turn. She waited, not too patiently, but she was learning that someone else had a right to speak at that moment. Then her turn came and she arose to the situation like a veteran, told her story while everyone listened, and then looked around and said, "Now whose turn is it?" She learned a valuable lesson that day. Haven't we all known adults whom we wish had been taught that lesson early in life?

The Importance of Parental Authority

A child who learns to yield to the loving leadership of his parents will one day submit to the other forms of authority which he will be confronted with later in life. Lack of respect for leadership produces rebellion and confusion. But most important, the child who yields to the loving authority of his parents will learn to yield to the loving leadership of his Heavenly Father.

Regardless of whether we like it or not, a little child relates his parents to God. He sees God just as he sees his earthly father. Is it any wonder that many children have a distorted picture of God? Parents' lives must reflect both authority and unlimited love so that they might best represent the divine nature of God. Children will learn of God's tender mercies through their parents' love for them. But our Heavenly Father is also a God of divine authority. To represent God with love and not with authority is as serious a misrepresentation as picturing God as absolute authority without love.

Therefore, a child who does not respect the authority of his parents and who has been allowed to sass and disobey their instructions can hardly be expected to submit readily to the authority of God. His first submission is yielding to his parents' authority, then to the leadership of his teachers, police, employers, and finally responding to the majestic authority of the Lord.

Children Learn by Watching

Far more important than what you say or try to teach is how you live. They learn best by watching and mimicking what you do. Dr. Howard Hendricks, professor at Dallas Theological Seminary, has said in his lectures on family living that you cannot impart what you do not know. You cannot teach your child what you have not experienced. Before a parent can develop a child's desire for spiritual things, he needs first to have a spiritual experience with Christ himself and then a plan for continual growth in the Lord. The greatest weakness in Christian homes is parents who try to teach their children principles contrary to what they themselves are living. This book can best benefit you if you first pause to look at your own life and your obedience to God. Then He can help you to become the kind of parent your child needs.

1. *Recognize* that Jesus Christ is God's only provision for man's sin.

> But God commendeth his love toward us in that,
> while we were yet sinners, Christ died for us.
> —Romans 5:8

In whom we have redemption through his blood, the forgiveness of sins, according to the riches of his grace, . . .

—Ephesians 1:7

2. *Repent* of your self-will.
Except you repent (turn from self-will to God's will), you shall all likewise perish.

—Luke 13:3

3. *Receive* Christ as Lord and Savior by turning your life over to Christ and making Him Lord of your life. When you invite Him in, He will cleanse you from your past sins and give you wisdom and guidance for your future.

But as many as received him, to them gave he power to become the sons of God, even to them that believe on his name.

—John 1:12

For whosoever shall call upon the name of the Lord shall be saved.

—Romans 10:13

4. *Remember* to let Jesus Christ direct the daily decisions of your life.

In all thy ways acknowledge him, and he shall direct thy paths.

—Proverbs 3:6

And be not drunk with wine, wherein is excess; but be filled (controlled) with the Spirit.

—Ephesians 5:18

When Christ controls your life, you will only permit your mind to think about those things that please Him—things which create the feelings of peace, love and happiness.

The secret to being the kind of parent God wants you to be is adherence to the above four principles: Recognize, repent, receive, remember. After taking these steps, the results will follow. You will "walk in the Spirit," which is a daily fellowshipping and communing with Christ. Galatians 5:16-17 says: "This I say then, Walk in the Spirit, and ye shall not fulfill the lust of the flesh. For the flesh lusteth against the Spirit and the Spirit against the flesh: and these are contrary the one to the other: so that ye cannot do the things that ye would.''

The old saying that "what you do speaks so loudly I can't hear what you say" is certainly true. How important it is then for moms and dads to be totally submitted to Jesus Christ, who will guide and direct what they do so it will not be contrary to what they say. When we are controlled by the Spirit, our thoughts, attitudes, actions and responses are all affected.

The heritage God has given to us in our children is certainly worth this act of obedience and dedication on our part. What greater reward can we receive than to see our children mature into good, law-abiding citizens, and best of all, men and women dedicated to the Lord Jesus Christ?

Why do Children Disobey?

There are six basic reasons why a child may become disobedient. Some children may have problems in all six areas while others will offend in only one.

1. *He does not know the Lord personally*. This is the primary reason for disobedience and also the most important. It is very important that parents introduce their child to Jesus Christ at an early age. A great deal of disobedience may be curbed when a child comes to Christ early in life because he will be at ease with himself. The transforming work of Christ makes a great difference in the total being of a youngster.

2. *He has been allowed to feed the sins of the flesh*. The child who is permitted to selfishly demand his own way and to feed the lust of the flesh will become rebellious toward the parent. When he is allowed to read whatever he wants, watch any TV program he chooses, and see any movie (regardless of its rating), he will rebel against God. It is outrageous what is being shown on the movie screens across the world to decay the minds and lives of the viewers, and the highest percentage of the audiences are young people. I cannot understand mothers, who carefully provide children with clean linens, healthy foods, sterilized and polished silverware, etc., then turn around and allow them to feed their minds in the garbage pits of the world

that will do more to contaminate and destroy their lives than sleeping on dirty linens or eating with dirty silverware.

Do you know what literature your child has been reading or what movies he has been seeing? One father decided for one month to watch every TV show his son watched and to see every movie at the theater his son went to see (that he was aware of). After twenty days the father decided he could not take any more. All this was affecting his thought life and attitudes, and he felt that he had stumbled on to why his son was becoming rebellious and argumentative. The wise parent will be aware of most of what the child feeds into his mind and will carefully set guidelines.

3. *He has lived with a lack of parental discipline.* In other words, permissive parents have not fulfilled the role of disciplinarians who love their children. The Bible says that the father is to be the head of the household and shall see that the children are brought up with discipline and instruction. All through the pages of Proverbs in the Old Testament there are numerous verses that admonish parents to discipline and train their children in the ways of wisdom. The mother is to be the assistant and fill in when the father is absent.

4. *He has not developed a spirit of submission.* Children best learn submission by watching—sons watching their fathers submit to God and daughters observing their mothers submit to their husbands. In order to be obedient, a child must have a submissive spirit. Disobedience must be corrected privately between the child and the parent, but restored publicly to the one he wronged. For instance, in our children's early years we had such an episode. Two of our children were walking home from the grocery store with their father. One the way, he discovered they each had a pocketful of little wrapped candies which he had not purchased. When he confronted them with the evidence, they both confessed to just helping themselves. The "rod of correction" was applied privately to each boy, and they all returned to the store to find the manager. The restoration came when they had to confess to him what they had done, ask his forgiveness, return the uneaten candy, and pay for the eaten ones out of their piggy banks. Correction like this

teaches a submissive spirit and a response to authority.

5. *He is struggling for the affection and attention of his parents*. Unfortunately, he discovers one of the quickest ways to get it is to be disobedient. To the child that is starving for love and attention, the consequences of disobedience are worthwhile just to gain the attention of his parents, even if it is only temporary. Many active parents are so involved with their own goals in life that they fail to see these struggles in their children. The best behaved children in school usually come from homes that are filled with family togetherness and lots of parental love.

6. *He has not been taught to respect authority*. The child who has not been trained to respect the authority of his parents will have great difficulty in respecting the authority of his teachers, law officers, employers, and, most of all, his Heavenly Father. Children may not respect authority because they do not see their mother being under submission to her husband or they do not see their father submitting to God. They will best learn by watching parental example. Where are the days when children were taught respect and answered, "Yes, sir" or "No, sir"? Instead, today answers are usually "uh-uh" or Unh-unh," if you are lucky. It is not the words that are so important but the respectful attitudes and the discipline that accompany the "Yes, sir" and "No, sir." Before a child can give respect, he has to recognize who has the authority, the power, and is the stronger being.

In closing this chapter, let me challenge you to begin now to respond to the six reasons a child disobeys. Examine the attitudes and responses of each of your children to see how they measure up to being obedient children. If they score high, then you are on the right path and are doing a good job in training up your child in the way he should go. Proper training does not require a great education, earthly possessions, or a high I.Q. It simply requires diligence to your calling and obedience to God.

During the Bicentennial summer, my husband and I, along with our two unmarried children, visited many of the historical sites in the East. At the Old Granary Cemetery in Boston, Massachusetts, we found an old tombstone that went back many years and the inscription could barely be seen. It was the marker for the graves of Benjamin Franklin's parents. It read as follows, "Josiah Franklin, 89, and Abiah, his wife, 85, lie here interred. They lived lovingly together in wedlock 55 years and without an estate or any gainful employment; by constant labor and honest industry, maintained a large family comfortably; and brought up thirteen children and seven grandchildren respectably. From this instance, Reader, be encouraged to diligence in thy calling, and distrust not Providence. He was a pious and prudent man, she a discreet and virtuous woman."

10

Discipline Is Not Just Punishment

My son, observe the commandment of your father,
And do not forsake the teaching of your mother;
Bind them continually on your heart;
Tie them around your neck.
When you walk about, they will guide you;
When you sleep, they will watch over you;
And when you awake, they will talk to you.
For the commandment is a lamp, and the teaching is light,
And reproofs for discipline are the way of life.

—Proverbs 6:20–23

Discipline is much more than punishment. So what is something you do for your child, not to your child. If you discipline them right, they will learn to guard or govern themselves. Discipline is part of the character you build into them, so they will be a light in a dark age.

Ephesians 6:4 (NASB), "And fathers, do not provoke your children to anger, but bring them up in the discipline and instruction of the Lord." This kind of discipline actually means creating a guide to help your children—having parents who define guidelines. It is more than a spanking or the loss of a privilege. Discipline is an ongoing investment in your character building relationship. In the name of discipline,

10

Discipline Is Not Just Punishment

My son, observe the commandment of your father,
And do not forsake the teaching of your mother;
Bind them continually on your heart;
Tie them around your neck.
When you walk about, they will guide you;
When you sleep, they will watch over you;
And when you awake, they will talk to you.
For the commandment is a lamp, and the teaching is
    light;
And reproofs for discipline are the way of life.
                              —Proverbs 6:20-23 (NASB)

Discipline is much more than punishment. Discipline is
something you do *for* your child, not *to* your child. If parents do
their training right, they will have to spank or correct a whole lot
less. Discipline is part of the character you build into your child
that will give him a way of life.

Ephesians 6:4 (NASB): "And, fathers, do not provoke your
children to anger; but bring them up in the discipline and
instruction of the Lord." This kind of training or discipline
means guiding a child to help him mature and develop
character with definite guidelines. It is more than giving him
orders and lists of rules. Discipline is to instruct, educate, guide
and train with faithful consistency. In the minds of many

people, discipline means punishment as a means of getting a youngster to behave. There are two aspects of discipline—preventive and corrective. Corrective measures are absolutely necessary at times, but preventive measures will build self-discipline into your child.

When you discipline your child, you are really training him to be a disciple. Dr. Henry Brandt says, "Parenthood is the process of making disciples of your children." In the early years he will be a disciple of you, his parents, and then as he matures and your teaching has laid the foundation, he will become a disciple of Jesus Christ. He will first be following your teaching and your example. How very important it is, then, that your teachings and your examples be closely parralleled to that of Christ. Does your child see an undisciplined parent who is trying to tell him how to be disciplined?

The parent who does not assume the responsibility of disciplining his child is treating the child as though he were illegitimate. Hebrews 12:8 (NASB): "But if you are without discipline, of which all have become partakers, then you are illegitimate children and not sons." An undisciplined child will feel like he does not belong to anyone and his self-esteem is adversely affected.

Discipline and love go hand in hand. How many times parents have told a child just before a sound spanking, "This hurts me more than it does you," and the child absolutely does not believe it. But when discipline and love are bound together, it does hurt the parent. It causes him to understand in a small way how the heart of God must ache when He has to discipline His children repeatedly. Effective discipline is impossible without love. Love without discipline is spineless and not genuine. Discipline without love is cold and militaristic, but when the two are joined together, the results are an effective tool for guiding, educating and correcting children.

Correction does not have a good effect on the child who hasn't been loved. The pain of punishment is not that effective. When the parent has developed a strong relationship with the child, then discipline that corrects will draw the parents and child closer together. His trust and admiration for his parent will reassure him in a time of correction that the parent is not doing it to seek revenge or to vent his anger. Rather, the child feels reassured that his parents truly care for him. Many times our own children would be extremely loving immediately after a spanking. Rather than feeling fear at such a time, they experienced relief in the confidence that they had been restored to a good standing with their parents. When children have been well loved by their parents, the correction ignites a responding love in them that makes them want to become mature like their parents and, most of the time, makes them want to please their parents and be in good standing with them.

The first two years of a child's life are the most important years in which the parents' love arouses a response in children. It is in that period that his trust or mistrust and his respect or disrespect for authority are determined. Every Christian parent desires that his child grow up to be a responsible citizen and a God-fearing Christian. It takes training every hour, day, week and month, to build these important factors into our children. No mother can afford the high risk of letting someone else train her child during these crucial years. She needs to be with them for most of the day in their early childhood, to be ready to give comfort, love, and instruction when they most need it. They need the interaction between mother and child that occurs during the day for proper development during the preschool years. For you mothers who are required to work because you are the sole support of your child, I would strongly urge you to enroll your little one in a good, Christian day-care center that will build Christian principles into his little heart. In addition, plan to spend as much of your non-working and non-sleeping hours as you can doing things together that will build trust and respect in him.

Good and bad behavior must be acknowledged for proper development and building self-esteem. Usually, when our children are good and well-mannered, we pay little or no attention to them. If they don't bother us, then we don't bother them. But when a child acts up, he gets our immediate attention. Instead of ignoring him when he is behaving well, try making a positive comment to him about something good he is doing, such as, "It's very enjoyable to have a quiet game to play." Or suggest to him how pleasant it is when everyone in the household is behaving and how he has made a real contribution to this good day.

Bad behavior can be helped in little children by reinforcing their good behavior. We can always find a reason to praise our children if we try hard enough. During a course of study in child development, I was assigned to do my laboratory work in a well-managed nursery school. One little boy in the school was a holy terror to his teacher and the other youngsters in his class. We looked for something for which we could praise him in an effort to motivate more cooperative behavior. It took some time and thinking, but finally we found a solution. Each afternoon there was a rest period, and one day he happened to be doing what he was supposed to be doing—resting. (He was probably exhausted from harassing his family the night before.) The teacher captured this moment by announcing after the rest period that this little fellow was the best rester in the class that day. His mother later told us that he had informed the entire family that evening at dinner that he was the best rester in the whole class, "the teacher said so." For the next several days he rested quietly, something which he had never done before. Children respond to praise and all children have some area in which they can be praised if we look hard enough.

How Effective Is Your Discipline?

It is wise to stand back and take a long look at the discipline you practice with your children and to carefully examine its quality and results. Unless a child understands what you expect of him, there is no way he can respond. The beginning of all discipline must begin with good, simple communication. The ultimate goal of parental discipline should be teaching the child self-discipline; communication is the beginning step to reach that goal.

A good, basic plan for discipline will have these definite characteristics. Ask yourself the following questions:

1. *Is it constructive?* Discipline should result in helping the

child rather than frustrating him. Proverbs 23:19 (NASB): "Listen, my son, and be wise, and direct your heart in the way."

2. *Is it creating wise choices?* Discipline should be guiding and educating a child to make wise choices of his own. In doing so, you are helping him become self-disciplined. Proverbs 19:20 (NASB): "Listen to counsel and accept discipline, that you may be wise the rest of your days."

3. *Is it consistent?* True discipline means being faithful and consistent to respond to disobedience. Discipline that is carried out one time and overlooked the next is not effective. Proverbs 29:17 (NASB): "Correct your son, and he will give you comfort; he will also delight your soul."

4. *Is it communicating love?* Discipline should spring from a heart of love for the child. It is also an assurance of belonging and being part of the family. Remember, "For those whom the Lord loves, He disciplines" (Hebrews 12:6, NASB).

5. *Is it confidential?* The child needs to know that the discipline is between the parent and himself and that it won't become the topic of conversation at the next neighborhood coffee party. Jeremiah 31:34b (NASB): "for I will forgive their iniquity, and their sins I will remember no more." This confidence also builds into the child the belief that you have forgiven him and now all is forgotten.

There are several methods of creative disciplining, and the wise parent needs to select the appropriate one for each occasion:

1. *You may deprive the child of something very important to him.* This will mean depriving him of a privilege to use or to do something that would be enjoyable for him. If Johnny takes the Play-Doh and consistently rubs it on the mahogany dining room table (and he is old enough to know better), then you might deprive him of the use of his Play-Doh for several days. Be sure you communicate to him that he has been told before (be sure that you have done this) not to put the clay on the furniture. Therefore, the best way to help him remember is to take away the privilege of using it for several days. This would serve as a reminder that Play-Doh is not to be used on the good furniture

but only at the special table designated by mother.

2. *You may isolate the child from his friends or in his room.* It is important that you do not send him to his room as if he had to stay there forever. The purpose is to encourage him to make a change in his behavior, and when he feels he is able to do this he can go back and play. Perhaps Sally has been an obnoxious tease with her friends to the point that she is causing constant turmoil. You should first communicate to her that she is causing trouble. Then inform her that she will have to go to her room and play by herself until she has decided that she can better control her actions. Always let her know that when she changes her behavior, she is welcome to go back and join her friends.

3. *You may let the child experience the natural consequences.* If you have communicated and it has not been effective, then you can turn to the unpleasant experience of allowing your child to reap the consequences. This cannot be allowed if it will cause severe harm to your child—you will have to weigh that potential. But remember, a little temporary physical pain is much better for our children than naggings and spankings that do not bring results. For instance, Mary has a cruel habit of pulling the cat's tail. You have communicated to her time and time again but to no avail. Then you finally decide that little Mary will have to experience for herself what happens when the cat's tail is pulled once too often. Even though she will undoubtedly suffer temporary pain, she will also learn through natural consequences that it is not wise to pull a cat's tail.

4. *You may use the "monetary reward system" for good and bad behavior.* This method has some very strong disadvantages. Probably the greatest is that it builds bad motivations. Some parents put charts on the wall that cover a week's worth of responsibilities. The children then accumulate points for completing what you expect them to do, such as making their beds, doing the dishes, taking out the trash, etc. When they neglect to do an assigned task, those points are subtracted from the week's total. The reward at the end of each week will be a certain amount of money for each point accumulated. But most

of us do not want our children to learn to do everything for money. They need to learn that there are certain things each member does just to carry his share of the load as a family member. This method is a glorified form of bribery and does not allow the parent to get at the root cause of the child's lack of motivation or disobedience. How much better it would be to occasionally present him with a special bonus for willing cooperation when he spontaneously shares in the household responsibilities.

5. *You may spank the child.* Spanking should be reserved for willful defiance or when other methods have been ineffective. Spanking should not be used to teach a child responsibility. When spankings are administered for defiant disobedience and they are given as the Bible teaches, then a little signal is sent to the child's brain that says, "I had better not do that again." There are right and wrong spankings. A wrong spanking would be a cruel, sadistic beating that is given in rage. This causes a child to be filled with anger and revenge and has not benefited him. A right spanking is given with a sound, positive approach. First, there needs to be communication on why the spanking will be given, and then it should be with a "rod" of correction and much love. One father had a paddle made with these words inscribed: "To my son with love." The Bible speaks clearly about the relationship of love and the "rod" of correction.

The Rod of Correction

"All discipline for the moment seems not to be joyful, but sorrowful; yet to those who have been trained by it, afterwards it yields the peaceful fruit of righteousness" Hebrews 12:11 (NASB). The Bible gives sufficient instruction on how to discipline a child. It always refers to a rod when it speaks of correcting children. Below is a list of some of the verses from Proverbs that speak about the rod of correction.

He who spares the rod hates his son,
But he who loves him disciplines him diligently.
—Proverbs 13:24, NASB
Foolishness is bound up in the heart of a child;

The rod of discipline will remove it far from him.
—Proverbs 22:15, NASB

Do not hold back discipline from the child,
Although you beat him with the rod, he will not die.
—Proverbs 23:13, NASB

You shall beat him with the rod,
And deliver his soul from Sheol.
—Proverbs 23:14, NASB

The rod and reproof give wisdom,
But a child who gets his own way brings shame to
his mother.
—Proverbs 29:15, NASB

I firmly believe that God did not intend parents to use their hand for correcting except for slapping the hands of a very young child. Since he cannot understand your words, he will understand when his hand gets slapped as it reaches out for the electric plug. The Bible continually refers to a "rod of correction." Children grow up to fear the rod and when the rod you use for correction is your hand, then he fears the hand that will reach out to him in love and affection. Also, when a rod is used it gives you time to cool off if you are angry. After you have announced that it is necessary to use it, send a child to find it and you will have time to confess your anger and plan your next step before you start spanking him. We would always send our children to get the "rod" which was a wooden spoon. It was surprising how that spoon was so difficult to find on many occasions, almost as though it had walked away.

When I have discussed this with other parents, I have found that many times they spanked spontaneously in anger with their hand, often striking the head, face or hand of the child. Any discipline done in anger is very ineffective and wrong. This is responding with hurt, disappointment, or revenge, and none of these will instruct or educate a child to do right. The Bible warns against angry men (or women) and tells us to avoid them.

Do not associate with a man given to anger;
Or go with a hot-tempered man.
—Proverbs 22:24, NASB

> An angry man stirs up strife,
> And a hot-tempered man abounds in transgression.
> > —Proverbs 29:22, NASB

> A fool always loses his temper,
> But a wise man holds it back.
> > —Proverbs 29:11, NASB

> He who is slow to anger has great understanding,
> But he who is quick-tempered exalts folly.
> > —Proverbs 14:29, NASB

> A quick-tempered man acts foolishly.
> > —Proverbs 14:17a, NASB

The parents who desire to practice effective discipline in their children will have to first get victory over their own anger and hot tempers. These parents need to confess that angry spirit to God and ask for help to change. "He who is slow to anger is better than the mighty, and he who rules his spirit, than he who captures a city" (Proverbs 16:32, NASB).

A proper place has been designated in the Scripture where the rod of correction should be used. God has prepared a place on each child's anatomy with a fatty tissue that will cushion a severe spanking so not to break bones or injure him. This area is at the base of the back and above the thighs situated directly on the back side of every child; they all come equipped with it. Proverbs refers to this spot and mentions its use.

> On the lips of the discerning, wisdom is found,
> But a rod is for the back of him who lacks
>   understanding.
> > —Proverbs 10:13, NASB

> Judgments are prepared for scoffers,
> And blows for the back of fools.
> > —Proverbs 19:29, NASB

> A whip is for the horse, a bridle for the donkey,
> And a rod for the back of fools.
> > —Proverbs 26:3, NASB

The wise parents will study the book of Proverbs for inspiration and guidance on disciplining their children. It is important to know what God says about correction and reproof, but it is not enough to just know about it. You have to put it into practice before it will be effective in the life of your child. "Poverty and shame will come to him who neglects discipline, but he who regards reproof will be honored" (Proverbs 13:18, NASB).

Guidelines for Disciplining

Dr. Thomas P. Johnson, a psychiatrist for the San Diego County Probation Department, has written the following guidelines for parents. They are worth reprinting and he was kind enough to grant permission.

1. Don't disapprove of what a child is—disapprove of what he does.

2. Give attention and praise for good behavior—not bad behavior.

3. Encourage and allow discussion, but remember it's the parents who should make the final decision.

4. Punishment should be swift, reasonable, related to the offense and absolutely certain to occur—it need not be severe.

5. Throw out all rules you are unwilling to enforce and be willing to change the rules if and when you think they need changing.

6. Don't lecture and don't warn—youngsters will remember what they think is important to remember.

7. Don't feel you have to justify rules, although you should try to explain them.

8. As your youngster grows older, many rules may be subject to discussion and compromise. The few rules you really feel strongly about should be enforced no matter what rules other parents have.

9. Allow a child to assume responsibility for his decisions as he shows the ability to do so.

10. Don't expect children to demonstrate more self-control than you do.

11. Be honest with your youngster—hypocrisy shows.

12. The most important factor in your youngster's self-image is what he thinks you think of him. His self-image is a major factor in how he conducts himself.

Temperaments Affect Discipline

The way parents discipline their children is often a reflection of their own temperament. That is why some parents are prone to be strict disciplinarians and other are apt to be permissive. Most people marry partners that are opposite temperaments, and this presents conflicts when it comes to disciplining children. The passive partner will be accused of being too easy going and the activist will be condemned because he is too strict. It is absolutely necessary for parents to come to an agreement on how they plan to discipline their children and then put into practice their united decision. There has to be a meeting of the minds to make discipline effective. Children will immediately recognize when their mom and dad do not agree, and they will begin to work one against the other.

Mary, for instance, had been disobedient and her father announced that she was on restriction for the whole weekend. I happened to be at their home when Mary told her mother she was going to a friend's house for the evening. The choleric father said, "I thought you were on restriction which means you are not allowed out of the house." The sanguine mother quickly interfered, "Oh, she is on restriction but she just has to leave a phone number where she is going." I watched the father turn red in the face and his eyes flash. If I had not been present, I am sure he would have exploded in rage. It was obvious that his wife was not reinforcing his discipline but rather was massaging it to suit herself. That daughter learned that day that her mom was an easy touch and that it was better to avoid going to her dad for permission. How much better it would have been if Mother had told Mary, "Your father and I have put you on restriction; therefore, you must stay home tonight."

Let's take a look at a common problem most homes are afflicted with and consider how the four different temperaments in parents would respond. Fighting between brothers and sisters is as natural as water running down hill. This seems to be a successful way that children have to worry parents. It usually starts with one child being the aggravator whether it be teasing or just "picking." It will not be long before words are going back and forth, then perhaps a shove or snatching away part of the game they were playing. Then the noise gets louder and sharper. Usually one will end up in tears and go running to the parents screaming out accusations. Who knows who is guilty and who has really started it? Chances are very good that neither are innocent. Parents respond so differently to scenes such as this.

The choleric parent is a strong disciplinarian and usually enforces any command that he gives. He will probably give one warning when he hears the battle begin to rage. After one warning to them to "Stop this minute or I will give you both a sound spanking" and nothing has changed, he will storm into the room, grab them one at a time and do just what he promised to do. He may even march them to the bedroom, lay them across the bed and whack them both so they know that they have been spanked. This parent will give little explanation except, "If I ever catch you fighting like that again, there will be more where that came from." The choleric will be the most consistent on discipline but will be lacking in the love to go with it.

The sanguine parent will warn them forty times to stop fighting. "Johnny stop that!"—"Johnny stop that!"—"If you don't stop that, I'll whip you!" and usually Johnny never gets whipped. Each time the warning will be louder and louder until finally, between the children fighting and the parents screaming, you have a sound that resembles the "1812 Overture." At last, this parent will rush into the room and either slap them across the back or spank them on the spot, but unfortunately he has waited until he was overcome with anger before he did anything. After the explosion has ended and the children are sobbing, the sanguine parent will begin to feel very badly because of his explosion and his spanking in anger. Many times he will try to make up to the children by handing out candy or some other sweet that will supposedly patch up everything. The sanguine will be inconsistent in his discipline. One day the children will be spanked for their actions and the next day the same action will be overlooked.

The melancholic parent will listen to the fighting and begin to feel as if he has failed. He will probably read into the scrap more than is there and will then go into the children on the verge of tears. "Why do you kids hate each other so?" or "Where have I failed?" or "Don't you kids realize what you are doing to me?" This parent will do a lot of talking and lecturing to these kids but will save the spanking for a last resort. Then they will tend to feel guilty and remorseful and will indulge in self-pity that the children would do this to them. Probably the end result will be an "Excedrin No. 59 headache."

The phlegmatic parent is the one who, whenever discipline is called for, tends to retreat from the scene of the action and hopes that his partner will solve the problem. He will either ignore the screaming or crawl into his shell as long as he can to tune out any trouble or violence. When he finally decides that the children may kill each other if something isn't done, this parent will crawl out of his shell long enough to calmly say, "I'm going to give you one more chance," or "What will your father (or mother) say?" Spanking is so foreign to the phlegmatic's nature that, if he is pressed into disciplining, he will probably set them on a chair or send them each to their bedroom. More than likely a phlegmatic mother will save the discipline until the father gets home. The phlegmatic father will probably retreat to the garage until the storm passes.

During our year of traveling around the world, we have lived and fellowshipped with hundreds of missionaries. One observation we made during that time was that some very well meaning missionaries were prone to raise their children in a permissive home. (There tends to be more melancholics and phlegmatics in the mission field than other temperaments.) The feeling seems to exist that their children are giving up so much to live on the mission field that the rebellion and disobedience must be overlooked. This spirit has been picked up by the children and they begin to feel sorry for themselves and indulge in self-pity. The result will be bitter young people who will always feel that they have been cheated in life.

How much better it would be if parents would dwell on the positive blessings in life and raise their children to respect the rod and its authority.

Self-Willed or Strong-Willed?

These two words sound very much alike yet there is a whole world of difference between them. Unfortunately, they have been used and misused so often that their true meanings have been mistaken.

The self-willed child has a weak will, not a strong one. He is driven by his appetites and the needs of the moment. His appetites control his will and his will dictates to his reason. This young person does pretty much as he pleases, spends his allowance on anything that catches his fancy, and cannot wait to be gratified when he desires something. A self-willed person is always manipulating and distorting reality to conform to his wishes. His selfishness is in full control and he has no consideration for God's will in his life.

A truly strong-willed child operates exactly the other way around. His reason directs his will and his will regulates his appetites. This young person can postpone the satisfaction of the present need in order to gain a higher and more permanent satisfaction at a later date. He has the ability to deny himself in order to reach higher goals. A strong will can accept the limitations of reality and live within them. He can withstand frustration and cope with it. All these are very good characteristics, but when he omits Christ from his life, these goals become selfish and count for nothing in eternity.

A strong-willed individual does not do what he wants to do, but what he sees must be done; a self-willed person does not possess the inner freedom to make that choice but is forced by his own needs to satisfy an immediate hunger. A strong-willed person possesses the ability to be independent of self; the self-willed person is totally enslaved to his own gratification.

You can help your child by looking at him with an honest eye and determining whether he is self-willed or strong-willed. These distinct features will begin to show at an early age. When you continually give in to his spontaneous wants and desires, you will be feeding your child's self-will. To develop a strong will, he must learn how to deny his selfish wants and wishes. But it is not enough to have just a strong will. That strong will can become selfish if its motivations are purely for self-gain. A lesson can be learned by considering what Jesus said in Matthew 16:24-25 (NASB), "If anyone wishes to come after Me, let him deny himself, and take up his cross, and follow Me. For whoever wishes to save his life shall lose it; but whoever loses his life for My sake shall find it." The self-willed person is only interested in his selfish desires and saving his life, and Jesus said he will lose it. But the one who is willing to deny himself and lose his life for the sake of Christ shall find his life. When the self-willed child receives Jesus as his Lord and Savior and is challenged to deny himself and follow Christ, then he can begin to develop the discipline required to be strong-willed without selfish motivations. The strong-willed child needs to be confronted with his need for a personal experience with Christ and the need to yield his own selfish goals and deny himself for the cause of Christ.

Discipline is so necessary in the life of each child, whether he is self-willed or strong-willed. It is important that parents properly discipline their children at a young age so they can be obedient to Christ and yield to His authority as they grow older.

11

Reaping The
Rewards Of Love

11

Reaping The
Rewards Of Love

"Of course, I love my kids," one father remarked. "I provide their food, clothing, and a roof over their heads. What more could a kid expect?"

A few days before, I had counseled with a young couple who had two children. I had just finished lecturing on the subject: "Loving Your Children Means Complete Involvement." As they approached me, I could see the look of disagreement in the wife's eyes. She immediately said, "Do you mean to tell me that I cannot always do what I want to do; that sometimes I have to give up my desires for my children? Isn't that asking an awful lot?" I knew that I had touched a real sore spot with this gal. Her husband stood behind looking rather embarrassed as I began to ask questions, because I knew there was a lot she wasn't telling me. As the story unfolded I realized that I was talking to a very selfish woman who had difficulty loving her children. She was so obsessed with herself that she could not be involved with her children. Loving and training children requires complete involvement. I used the example of the Heavenly Father's relationship to His children. How neglected we would be if He provided only air to breathe, some food and clothing. Instead He becomes completely involved with us. His love extends to our professions in life, marriage relationships, hurts and disappointments, joys and achievements, sicknesses and health, and even our wants and desires.

Matthew 7:9-12 (NASB): "Or what man is there among you, when his son shall ask him for a loaf, will give him a stone? Or if he shall ask for a fish, he will not give him a snake, will he? If you then, being evil, know how to give good gifts to your children, how much more shall your Father who is in heaven give what is good to those who ask Him! Therefore whatever you want others to do for you, do so for them, for this is the Law and the Prophets." The Holy Spirit seemed to take my feeble words and use them to prick her conscience. I watched this hardened and hostile woman become softened and moved to tears. The three of us put our arms around each other as she prayed that the Lord would forgive her of her selfishness and teach her to love her children even as Christ loved her.

Another young mother asked me, "How can children enrich a marriage when they limit your freedom, interrupt your conversations, spend your money, invade your privacy, exhaust your strength, and shatter your nerves?" I could agree that this may be the case in some families, but I know many homes where this is not true and that certainly isn't true of ours. In spite of all the limits, interruptions, expenses and strains that go with parenthood, I firmly believe that children add new depth and richness to the pleasures of marriage. Probably the greatest difference is the attitude with which you face it. The mother who says, "What can a family give to me?" will get headaches, exhaustion and shattered nerves. But the mother who wants to know "What can I give my family?" is going to reap the rewards of love and happy parenthood.

In the story of Suzanna Wesley's life it is reported that she spent one hour a week of uninterrupted time with each of her fifteen children. Then when each one graduated from the home, she spent that hour in prayer for them. What a spirit of living! She certainly had many rewards to reap from the love she bestowed on her children.

Reaping What You Sow

In order to reap the rewards of love, you must first sow the seeds of love. Many of the seeds may be sown sacrificially, but when the time comes to reap the rewards the sacrifices will be forgotten. After all, any worthwhile accomplishment in life will require a sacrifice on our part. The "seeds of love" will mean complete involvement with your child during the few years you have to sow before you can begin to reap.

LISTENING—How you listen to your child will say one of two things to him. It will say, "Don't bother me; I'm too busy," or, "I am not too busy to listen to what you have to tell me." The first will cause a child to withdraw deeper into his own solitude, and he will begin to think that he is a nuisance and not important enough to be listened to. The second gives the child the security of being respected and considered an important human being and worthy to be heard. Paul Tournier, noted author and Swiss physician has said, "It's impossible to overemphasize the immense need humans have to be really listened to."

Someone has said that good listening requires two things: concentration and restraint. True listening involves concentrating on what is being said, what is not being said or what they are "skirting around," and what they are really trying to tell the listeners. Listening also requires restraint from reacting or over-reacting and from interrupting or criticizing what is being said.

Your ability to listen will also help you to evaluate the value of your own words because much of what they say will be a reflection of your own.

COMMUNICATING— You will communicate acceptance or criticism, love or rejection, by how you talk to your child. The tone of your voice, the look of your eye, or the way you touch or stroke the child will speak more loudly than what you actually say.

There is a great need for fathers to be willing to communicate spiritual truths to the family. (In homes where there is no father, or the father is not interested in teaching Biblical truths, then the responsibility falls on the mother.) Blessed is the child who is raised in a home where he is loved enough to have someone take an interest in his spiritual well-being to give him basic truths to live by.

We were greatly impressed by what we saw in one local church in Florida. At the close of a seminar we held in the church, the pastor made the announcement that all the men who had led in family devotions during the past week were invited to the front for a brief meeting. I watched while over three hundred men moved toward the front to meet with the pastor for ten to fifteen minutes. It was an uncommon sight and my curiosity got the best of me. When the pastor was finished, I asked him how he had started that program. He explained that six months earlier he had realized that the men in his church were not communicating scriptural truths to their family, so one Sunday evening he announced that he would like to meet with any men up in front who had led in family devotions during the past week. Twenty men met with him who could say they had done this. He continued each Sunday to meet with any men who had done it the previous week. The only requirements to attend this brief meeting of instruction, inspiration and encouragement were to lead in family devotions during the week before. They were not making commitments to be willing to do it nor expressing their good intentions to do it; they were there because they had already done it. Six months later the number had grown to over three hundred homes who were communicating daily spiritual truths to their families. That church and community will undoubtedly reap the benefits from such effective communication.

DISCIPLINING— This is such an important seed that one chapter has already been given to it (Chapter Ten), but it must be listed in the seeds to be sown. Discipline and love should never be separated because they involve a relationship between the parent and child. There should be equal love and discipline from both parents. We see the example of Esau in Genesis 25-27. He was not disciplined and was loved by only one parent. They reaped what they sowed. Genesis 26:35 says that Esau and his wife "brought grief to Isaac and Rebekah."

When discipline is properly utilized it gives the family stability. Children need to understand the rules of the family because it will give them security as they function daily within the limits it provides. Proper discipline serves as a fence so that children can know how far they can go.

I found it very amusing recently as we traveled through Africa to observe that wild animals could have a built-in sense of proper discipline. We were driving through a wild game reserve in Kenya when we came upon a large herd of elephants. There were elephants of all sizes, from the very large males to small baby elephants. As we pulled off the road to watch them as they approached, it soon became obvious which one was the mother of the youngest. She sensed that we were a potential danger and wanted her baby to stay with the herd. In typical, childlike fashion the young wanted to wander off to the side. She snorted at him to get his attention and he politely ignored her. Finally, after her warning, she walked alongside and whacked him on the rear end with her trunk. He knew exactly what she wanted him to do and he turned and obediently joined the group. Moments later I saw her walk alongside of him and rub him with her huge body as if it were a stroke of love. That parent and child seemed to have a good relationship with a proper balance of love and discipline.

FORGIVING — They learn forgiveness by watching you. How do you forgive their mother? their father? the person who wronged you? In each situation you are silently teaching them by your example. When they have hurt or disappointed you, are you able to forgive and forget it? When you do not forgive and forget, then you carry a grudge which becomes a wedge that divides and separates.

I observed a father who responded to his son with bitter hurt and disappointment. The boy had been disobedient and deserved punishment, but because the dad reacted out of hurt rather than trying to help the son, it became a wedge that separated their relationship. He took away five very special privileges over the three summer months that were very harsh. Any one privilege denied would have been severe, but because of the dad's own hurt feelings, he overreacted. So for three months of summer vacation the boy had little to do but sit in his room and feel sorry for himself. Out of it grew bitterness and resentment and the whole experience mushroomed way out of proportion. How much better it would have been if the father had disciplined the boy in love rather than hurt and done it quickly instead of spread over three months. He then could have told the son that he had forgiven him and all would be forgotten. Such a challenge would have helped the boy to profit from the mistake and do better. Any boy could respect his father for that kind of discipline, and most would respond with a desire to improve and not hurt his dad again.

RESPECTING — Love includes respecting your child's judgment and decisions. They may not be the same as yours. Of course they will be immature and inexperienced, but at least give them consideration. Let him know that they are worth being evaluated. At certain times there would be great benefit to allow him to follow a decision he has made if you are sure it will not be harmful to him. You will be helping to build his self-confidence and self-esteem.

The greatest respect you can show your child is in his personal rights. Every child has rights that are due him and the parent who loves with involvement will consider and respect them. His rights can be just a simple explanation, but they are, nevertheless, very important to him.

Last summer while visiting the East coast of the United States, my family saw a firsthand example of a child's rights being violated. Our two college-age young people, my husband and I were waiting in the long lines to see the Statue of Liberty in Long Island Harbor. It was a hot, summer afternoon and the line was moving very slowly. A little family stood in front of us with two small children. Those little children were restless and warm and not too happy about standing in line. The father left the line just long enough to go to the refreshment stand and came back with two ice cream cones for the children. They settled right down—such contentment! The entire line seemed to be more happy when the children were. Then the line began to move and shortly we were just inside the door. Immediately upon entering there was a large sign posted that read, ABSOLUTELY NO FOOD OR DRINKS PERMITTED INSIDE. The young mother read the sign and quickly responded by snatching the two ice cream cones out of the clutches of her children and dropped them into the trash can with no explanation given. She could read the sign, but the two children could not. All they knew was that one moment they were enjoying an ice cream cone and the next moment it was taken away and disposed of. They exploded in protest and we toured the Statue of Liberty to the sound of two children crying out in rage because their rights had been violated. At one point halfway through the monument the mother stopped and spanked them both for crying. Indeed, it was unfortunate because it seemed that the wrong person was being spanked. If parents would take the time to look at things through a child's eyes and respect his rights, much confusion could be avoided.

No Greater Joy

There could be a longer list of the "seeds of love" that should be sown, but I have shared enough to impress you that it takes a sacrifice of your time, energy, interest and attitudes. When you plant a garden, it takes a sacrifice on your part to prepare the soil, sow the seed, water, weed, spray for bugs, etc. But the day you pick that first ear of fresh corn, prepare it to be served at the dinner table, and taste that delicious, sweet, tender ear of corn you forget the sacrifice of time, energy, and plain, hard work. And so it is with your children. When you reap the first picking of rewards and you get that first sweet taste of satisfaction from a job well done, you no longer remember the sacrifices that it took to accomplish that goal. When you see your son or daughter march across that high school graduation platform to receive the diploma that represents 12 or 13 years of training, at that moment your heart is swelled with joy and you do not remember the unpleasant things in the past. The nights of little sleep when they were sick, the confrontations that made your heart ache, the day they broke several pieces of your best china, or even the large sums of money that it has taken to raise that child all seem to fade into the background as you get that first sweet taste of satisfaction from a job well done and a goal accomplished.

But lasting joy does not come to the parents in seeing their children successful in this world if they are not walking in the truth. Everyone wants happiness for their children, and the way of happiness is obeying the principles of God. III John 4 (NASB): "I have no greater joy than this, to hear of my children walking in the truth." There is no greater joy than knowing that your children are pleasing the Lord and walking in the Spirit. It is the parent who plays the greatest human role in helping the child accomplish that goal.

THE END

Other Good
Harvest House Reading

TEENAGERS: PARENTAL GUIDANCE SUGGESTED
by *Rich Wilkerson*

With dynamic impact, well-known youth speaker Rich Wilkerson has captured for every sincere parent the secrets of achieving a fulfilling relationship with his teen. Honest answers for the tough issues we face with our children. Formerly *Hold Me While You Let Me Go.*

PARENTS TALK WITH YOUR CHILDREN
by *V. Gilbert Beers*

One of life's most intimate human relationships is that of parent and child. Nothing is more important for a parent than knowing how to reach the heart of his or her child. Nothing is more important for a child than having parents who share their hearts.

V. Gilbert Beers, father of five and bestselling author of *Little Talks About God and You*, shares his experiences and insights and challenges parents to develop the kind of *talking relationship* with their children that will bring a lifelong friendship.

PARENTS IN CONTROL
Bringing Out the Best in Your Children
by *David Rice*

Getting your children under control is not as difficult as it might seem. *Parents in Control* explores: 1) How do parents get out of control? and 2) How to bring out the best in your child. Written for every parent, whether single or married, *Parents in Control* combines insight with a "nuts and bolts" approach to solving family problems.

PARENTHOOD WITHOUT HASSLES—Well Almost
by *Kevin Leman*

You will find this book to be practical in every sense of the word. Its aim is to teach parents how to better understand themselves and their children and how to create situations in the home conducive to Christian growth and learning.

STRESS IN THE FAMILY
How to Live Through It
by *Tim Timmons*

Inner and outer stress factors can destroy you and your family! Understanding the pressure you tolerate daily, you will discover *action-steps* that use stress to build you up rather than break you down.

Other Books by the LaHayes:

THE SPIRIT-CONTROLLED WOMAN
by *Beverly LaHaye*

This bestselling book gives the Christian woman practical help in understanding herself and the weaknesses she encounters in her private life and in her relationships with others. Told from a woman's point of view, this book covers every stage of a woman's life.

HOW TO STUDY THE BIBLE FOR YOURSELF
by *Tim LaHaye*

This excellent book provides fascinating study helps and charts that will make personal Bible study more interesting and exciting. A three-year program is outlined for a good working knowledge of the Bible.

Notes:

Dear Reader:

We would appreciate hearing from you regarding this Harvest House nonfiction book. It will enable us to continue to give you the best in Christian publishing.

1. What most influenced you to purchase *How to Develop Your Child's Temperament*?
   - ☐ Author
   - ☐ Subject matter
   - ☐ Backcover copy
   - ☐ Recommendations
   - ☐ Cover/Title
   - ☐ _____

2. Where did you purchase this book?
   - ☐ Christian bookstore
   - ☐ General bookstore
   - ☐ Department store
   - ☐ Grocery store
   - ☐ Other

3. Your overall rating of this book:
   - ☐ Excellent ☐ Very good ☐ Good ☐ Fair ☐ Poor

4. How likely would you be to purchase other books by this author?
   - ☐ Very likely
   - ☐ Somewhat likely
   - ☐ Not very likely
   - ☐ Not at all

5. What types of books most interest you?
   (check all that apply)
   - ☐ Women's Books
   - ☐ Marriage Books
   - ☐ Current Issues
   - ☐ Self Help/Psychology
   - ☐ Bible Studies
   - ☐ Fiction
   - ☐ Biographies
   - ☐ Children's Books
   - ☐ Youth Books
   - ☐ Other _____

6. Please check the box next to your age group.
   - ☐ Under 18
   - ☐ 18-24
   - ☐ 25-34
   - ☐ 35-44
   - ☐ 45-54
   - ☐ Over 54

Mail to: Editorial Director
Harvest House Publishers
1075 Arrowsmith
Eugene, OR 97402

Name _____

Address _____

City _____ State _____ Zip _____

Thank you for helping us to help you in future publications!